Life Beyond the Pandemic
A Practical New Journey Handbook

Learn Real World, Spiritual and
Useful Tools to Rebuild, Restart and
Have a Happy, Prosperous and Joyous Life!

ORESTE J. D'AVERSA

PUBLISHER'S NOTE

This book is designed to provide accurate and authoritative information in regard to the subject matter covered. It is sold with the understanding that neither the author nor publisher is engaged in rendering psychological, legal, or other professional service. If psychological, legal, professional advice or other expert assistance is required, the services of a professional, in that field, should be sought. The principles and concepts presented in this book are the opinions of the author and based on his interpretations of the aforementioned principles. Neither the author nor publisher are liable or responsible to any person or entity for any errors contained on this book, website, or for any special, incidental, or consequential damage caused or alleged to be caused directly or indirectly by the information contained in this book or website. Any application of the techniques, ideas and suggestions in this book is at the reader's sole discretion and risk.

Copyright © Oreste J. D'Aversa, 2020. All rights reserved.

No part of this publication may be reproduced, redistributed, taught, stored in a retrieval system, or transmitted, in any form or by any means, electronic, mechanical, photocopy, recording, or otherwise, without the prior written permission of the publisher.

FIRST EDITION

ISBN: 978-1-952294-03-7 (Paperback)

Library of Congress Number: 2020908360

Published by: *Cutting Edge Technology Publishing*.

About the Author

Oreste "Rusty" D'Aversa has over twenty years' experience in the various functions of corporate work (Selling, Pre/Post-Sales Support, Training, Consulting, Technical Support, and Customer Service) predominately in the Technology industry.

He also has over 15 years' experience as a "Solopreneur" being a "One Person Industry" as a Small Business Coach, Consultant, Trainer, Author, Speaker, Seminar Leader, Public Speaking Coach, Job Search Coach and University Lecturer.

He is also known as Rev. Oreste J. D'Aversa ("Reverend Rusty") is an Inter-Faith (All-Faiths) Minister ordained by The New Seminary in New York City, NY. He is a Spiritual Coach, Guide, Teacher, and Counselor helping people on their spiritual path and with their life purpose.

He has appeared on television and radio as well as having his work featured in various newspapers, journals and websites discussing his expertise in various business related and personal growth subject matter and has authored numerous books, manuals, articles, and audio CDs.

To learn more about him you can go to his websites:

www.LifeBeyondTheCoronavirus.com
www.MetroSmallBusinessCoaching.com
www.GodLovesYouAndMe.org
www.HealingHolesInMySoul.com

Table of Contents   Page

Introduction 1

PART I: The Prologue – The Game Plan.................................... 5

   Chapter 1: First Things First..7

   Chapter 2: Getting Back to Basics 13

   Chapter 3: The Reality of Starting Over 17

   Chapter 4: The Game Plan for Your New Life 19

PART II: The Spiritual: (Our Life Force)................................. 21

   Chapter 5: New Beginning Quotes..23

   Chapter 6: Why Are We Here on This Beautiful Planet 25

   Chapter 7: Being Human – What Does It Really Mean 27

   Chapter 8: Some Exercises to Make Your Creativity Flow!.....35

   Chapter 9: A Little Bit of Spiritual Stuff to Help
      You on Your Journey 51

   Chapter 10: Spiritual Guidance: Finding Your
      Purpose from Some Interesting Sources.........................57

   Chapter 11: Prosperity: What is the True Meaning? 61

   Chapter 12: You Have the Power to Create Your
      Perfect Life Experience..63

PART III: The Emotional (Our Emotional Heart) 71

   Chapter 13: More New Beginning Quotes.............................73

   Chapter 14: Emotional Baggage –
      The Personal Clutter that Hold You Back 75

   Chapter 15: Public Service - Service to Others........................85

   Chapter 16: What's Your True Passion in Life? 89

Chapter 17: How Would Like to Live Your Life?......................93

Chapter 18: Finding Your Path to Where You Want to Go.....97

PART IV: The Mental (Our Mind) 101

Chapter 19: Even More New Beginning Quotes 103

Chapter 20: The Power of Our Minds 105

Chapter 21: What are Your Personal Gifts,
Talents and Attributes?..115

Chapter 22: Uncover All of Your Education and Skills 117

PART V: The Physical (Our Body) 121

Chapter 23: Yes, Even More New Beginning Quotes............123

Chapter 24: Eating Right, Exercise and Mother Nature........125

Chapter 25: The Real World: How Do I Move Forward
with My Life?..129

Chapter 26: Your REAL Job – Learn How to Find It!.............133

Chapter 27: Yes, You Can Have a Job and Live
Your Life Purpose 179

Chapter 28: Should I be an Entrepreneur and
Run My Own Business?..183

Chapter 29: Business Tools to Help You with Your Business 239

PART VI: Epilogue Putting it All Together 277

Chapter 30: Your Life Purpose Statement –
Let the Whole World Know Who You Really Are! 279

Chapter 31: Your Life Master Plan –
Planning Your Work and Working Your Plan 285

Chapter 32: Enjoy and Celebrate Your Life's Purpose
and Celebrate Your Life! 291

Chapter 33: Now Let's Get Back to Our Better New,
    Better and Prosperous Lives! 295
Conclusion 299

PART VII: Resources 305
Resources 307
Footnotes 321
Bibliography.. 323

Dedication

I dedicate this book to all people that have lost everything in their lives and had to start over again. May the new beginnings in their lives bring them to better places than they were before and make them stronger; physically, mentally, emotionally, and spiritually and may they become a prosperous (in every way) and better people for having gone through the experience. May their wisdom, knowledge and true grit be "paid forward" to all the people that they meet on their journey so they too may have the courage, strength, and fortitude to continue their new journeys as well and live better lives for doing so.

Preface

I am writing this book at a time when the world is experiencing one of the worst pandemics in human history and definitely one of the worst in my lifetime. As I have written books in the past where I know how the book will end by the time I reach the end of writing this book I have no idea where the world will be and what the global conditions will be at that time. One thing I believe to be true is that there will be a "new normal". As I think about these words "new" and "normal" what are they really going to mean in the near future and moving forward in our lives? What is going to be "new" and what will "normal" look like? I do suspect that life as we knew before the pandemic will be different. How different and what way different that will remain to be seen. Somethings will not change, people still need to work, eat, need a place to live, taxes have to be paid, the bills will keep coming and the various other life surviving things will keep on happening and life will go on. I do believe that people may need to reassess their lives from the ground up as the world may be somewhat different. Who am I really? Why am I here? What's my true purpose in life? What's really important in my life? Who is really important in my life? Where do I go from here? How do I make a living? Do I find another job, or do I start my own business? And a host of other life affirming important questions.

I don't know what things will remain the same and what things will be radically different. Regardless of what will happen I am writing this book to offer people a "Swiss Army Knife" of sorts to have various tools for the different aspects of their lives. To be able to handle whatever may come your way there will be tools in this book to help you on your journey. We all are multifaceted human beings composed of: The Spiritual (the life force that keeps us animated as human beings), The Emotional (the "heart centered" part of being human), The Mental (the part of our being we call the Mind) and The Physical (our physical bodies). I believe if we are going to be prosperous in the new reality of a post pandemic world, all facets of being human must work at their optimal levels. If there is any "dis-ease" (an out of balance situation) in any of the above it will impact how we move forward. This will lead to examining all parts of our lives, to keep what works and to let go of what does not serve us any longer.

While not a natural disaster in the traditional sense to a weather event, earthquake and such, the pandemic is a life changing event nonetheless and in being so it's important to be in touch and stay in touch with family, friends, ensure your housing situation is secure and know the location of all important documents. [1]

A new journey awaits us all. As with any journey it's always best to pack what you will need and have a plan as to where you are going and what you will be doing along the way.

Introduction

This handbook is designed to give the reader tools for the new era that is being fostered in by the advent of the pandemic known as the Coronavirus (a.k.a. COVID-19) and the effects it will have on the modern age. Hopefully, it will make all of us think and behave in a new way, a better way that will usher in a better quality of life for everyone. The methods, tools and techniques in this handbook are not designed to be a "quick fix" or "flash in the pan" sensationalism but are meant to help people build long, meaningful, and prosperous changes in our lives. There are no "get rich quick" or "pyramid schemes" here; just tried and true ways to create, build and live a better, prosperous, and joyous life. In this handbook you will be taught "how to fish" so to speak (from the famous quote: "Give a Person a Fish, and You Feed Them for a Day. Teach a Person TO Fish, and You Feed Them for a Lifetime"), you will learn skills that will last a lifetime.

No matter what happens in your future you will be able to do what you need to do to get back on your feet – spiritually, emotionally, mentally, physically, and financially. I also want to share this quote from the movie Heartbreak Ridge. In the film, Marine Sergeant Thomas "Gunny" Highway (played by Clint

Eastwood) said, *"You're Marines now. You adapt. You overcome. You improvise. Let's move!"*. This handbook will provide you the tools you need to do just that – adapt, overcome, and improvise.

This handbook will have seven parts to it which are as follows:

Part I: The Prologue – The Game Plan

Part II: The Spiritual (Our Life Force)

Part III: The Emotional (Our Emotional Heart)

Part IV: The Mental (Our Mind)

Part V: The Physical (Our Body)

Part VI: Epilogue – Putting it All Together

Part VII: Resources

In **Part I: The Prologue – The Game Plan** - I will layout a "New Life Blueprint" of what a new way of living will look like and how it will be of benefit to you.

In **Part II: The Spiritual (Our Life Force)** – Spirituality has long been considered something for those people that had were considered not to be religious but wanted to believe in something outside of themselves. The fact is we are all spiritual beings and we are all here for a reason and each one of us has a "life purpose" to fulfil.

In **Part III: The Emotional (Our Emotional Heart)** – Many of us carry "emotional baggage" that is holding us back from reaching our true potential.

It's time we let go of this baggage and to be good to ourselves and to others.

In **Part IV: The Mental (Our Mind)** – We have this powerful thing (I prefer to think of it as a body part) called "The Mind" yet we are not taught how to use it to it's full potential. We also need to understand all of our "natural gifts", skills and abilities to see how we can make a difference in our own life and that of the lives of others.

In **Part V: The Physical (Our Body)** – Our bodies must be taken care of, if they are to last the time period we are on this planet. We're also here to live in the real world, to take care of this world and contribute to it in a meaningful way. Make a proper living and enjoying the fruits of our labors for ourselves, family and friends.

In **Part VI: Epilogue – Putting it All Together** – It's time to put into motion the "New Life Blueprint" to have a better life and to make the world a better place for all people.

In **Part VII: Resources** – Tools, websites, and other resources to make it all happen.

I do suggest you purchase a dedicated notebook and writing instrument to document your journey to your new and prosperous life as there will be exercises through this handbook to help to achieve all of your professional and personal goals.

As I previously mentioned, I don't know what the end of this handbook will look like, but what I do know is that when this pandemic is declared to be finally over, life will be different. How different, we will all know together. One thing is clear, the more "tools" you have in your "personal toolbox" the more prosperous you, your family and your friends will be and the more opportunities you will have.

I wish you much prosperity, good health and happiness on your new life journey!

PART I:

The Prologue

The Game Plan

NOTES

Chapter 1

First Things First

With the advent of the current pandemic some people may be completely starting over in their lives. Losing everything - careers, finances and even loved ones. For many the experience may be comparable to a natural disaster and in being such should be treated the same to start the rebuilding process of a person's life.

It's important not to lose sight that you can rebuild your life and that some changes may be necessary, but it can be done, and you will be better off for the new transformation. Let's start with the important foundational things in one's life:

Housing: It may be necessary to downsize your living arrangements to save money. If you own a house you need to rent for a while until you get back on your feet financially.

Relocation: Does it make sense to relocate to a different place where you could earn a living? It's a very big decision with all kinds of costs associated with it. And the costs are upfront and hidden along the way. The upfront costs of moving tend to be straight forward. The hidden costs are the ones that are the surprising ones and not expected. For example, you have a fairly new car with low mileage, and you think it will last another five years. However, on the way to your new location, you blow the engine. There's just one cost you weren't counting on to add to your relocation.

Finances: Make sure you have your finances squared away so you can get access to money when you need it. Check with your financial advisor to see if it makes sense to dip into retirement savings and 401k and such. Obviously, you don't want to use the funds as they were set away for your retirement and there is a very good chance that there will be financial penalties involved in doing so, but if you need the funds to survive, you need the funds to survive. Having been there myself I can assure you it's the very last thing you want to do as the financial penalties for early withdrawal are not pleasant at all!

Work and Career: Can you go back to the same work you used to do? Is that type of work even available to go back to? What happens if the pandemic wiped out that type of work locally, geographically, or even nationally? Then what? It might be time to think about a different line or work or even a different career path? If you do change the line of work or career, what skills and education are you going to need to get the new job? Though not impossible, it's a bit of a challenge to go from being an accountant to be a dentist. Or from being carpenter to being computer programmer. What skills and education do you possess and what jobs are going to be available? Are you going to need to go back to school, be it a "brick and mortar" or online schooling to get the necessary skills and education you will need to work in a post pandemic world?

Family and Friends: How is the post pandemic world going to affect your family and friends? Is your family going to split up in order to find work? Some family members may find work locally while others may have to find work in other states. The same may hold true for your friends and their families. Do you stay where you are, or do you go with them and the respective costs associated with the relocation?

Health: Are you and your family in good health? And all that goes along with that. You may be in a part of the country that has excellent health resources and if you relocate will that hold true in your new location? Do you have family members that cannot be moved due to age, quality of care issues or simply put, they will not move from all they know - family, friends, doctors, shopping, etc.**?**

Education: Are you in a part of the country that offers an exceptionally good school system? How will moving away from that school system impact you and your family?

The point of this chapter is ensure that the important things in your life have been thought about before you start making any major decisions and changes to your life and the lives of your family members. The post pandemic world may mean some serious and substantial changes to one's life and the lives of family members and friends as well.

EXERCISE: CURRENT LIFE INVENTORY. Take a look at the categories above and write down where you are and the impact (and costs) to make changes for you and your family. Costs may not always be financial either. Is learning new skills and education to stay where you are (and maybe even getting a better job) worth more to you than relocating (and all the costs that go with that) your entire family based on your current skills? What's all that worth to you?

NOTES

NOTES

Chapter 2

Getting Back to Basics

When starting over it is an exceptionally good time to get back to basics in all aspects of your life: Spiritually, Emotionally, Mentally, Physically and Financially. It is a time to rebuild one's life to make it even better than before. As with building a new house, a builder would start with a new foundation to build an even better house than before. While some things can be re-used and others re-purposed, everything needs to be examined and evaluated to see what works, what doesn't work any longer and what needs to be replaced.

In the area of Spirituality, are you a spiritual person? Religious person? Both? Neither? What are your personal beliefs in this area? Do you believe in a Supreme Being? Do you have <u>any</u> beliefs in these areas? There are no right or wrong answers here but things to ponder in moving forward in your life. Believing in things outside of yourself, especially of a high power in nature, can and will get through different times.

In the area of the Emotional aspects of your life, do you have a healthy love for yourself and others? Do you see service to others as helping others as well as helping yourself? Do you have healthy personal relationships in your life? Are there any unresolved emotional issues that may be holding you back from reaching all you can be as a person? This is a good time to start "doing the work on your emotional self". Personally, I had issues with my parents that held my life back for the longest time. As I did the self-work and released much of the "pain, anger and sorrow" of my past, I feel lighter and my life is opening up to new experiences, new people and my heart is open to being happier than I was before I did the work.

Mentally, what are you putting into your mind? Our minds work similar to a computer – Garbage in and garbage out. Are your filling your mind with "mental trash" by listening to those that spew hate, violence and misinformation? Or are you filling your mind professionally and personally with information that is going to make you a better person – more valuable to the business marketplace and more valuable to the world?

Physically, are you eating right, exercising, and taking care of your physical body? Eating healthy and unprocessed foods? And yes, we can spoil yourselves on occasion ☺ Trying to recycle more to help our planet. Donating things we no longer use instead of throwing them out. Helping those less fortunate than us by donating food, money, our time to help the world be a better place.

Last but not least, Financially. How's your financial wellbeing? Have savings for the future? Any emergency situation? For your retirement? Maybe it's time to be reevaluating all of your finances and your financial future as well**?.**

Getting back to basics is not very sexy, but it does provide a strong platform to build an even better life than before. By making even the smallest adjustments to the basic things in our lives sometimes other and major parts things just fall into place all by themselves to make our lives even better.

EXERCISE: Write down everything you are grateful for – and I mean everything on all levels – Spiritually, Mentally, Emotionally, Physically, Financially, etc. Write until you can't write anymore and then write some more. Put it down for a few days and write even more. The point of the exercise is to be grateful for all of the things and blessings you <u>do have</u> and not focus and what you don't have.

NOTES

Chapter 3

The Reality of Starting Over

Starting over really stinks and I will be the first person to tell you that! Starting over at 60 was not something I was planning on doing in this lifetime and continues to be not the greatest thing in the world that I have experienced. Another added bonus is having lost just about everything financially is not a great joy either! So I speak from experience on the subject. With that said, it's not the worst thing in the world either to go through. Yes, there are many "trials and tribulations" to go through but there are also many exciting new things happening as well.

Starting over intentionally (your choice) or not intentionally (not your choice) is challenging at best and just plain lousy at it's worst. Unfortunately, it is a fact of life for many people for a host of different reasons: natural or man-made disasters, health issues, family situations and the current situation – the pandemic As the saying goes, "Life goes on…" is of little solace when you are stuck in the muck and mire of daily modern day survival. Trying to make a living, trying to make a living with new rules on how to make a living, pay bills, taking care of family, extended family, pets, and the list goes on and on…

The late great actress Elizabeth Taylor has a great quote for this time in one's life, she said - *"You just do it. You force yourself to get up. You force yourself to put one foot in front of the other, and God d--n it, you refuse to let it get to you. You fight. You cry. You curse. Then you go about the business of living. That's how I've done it. There's no other way."* Being a Minister at first I found the quote a bit offensive, but the more I pondered it (notwithstanding the profanity), the more I realized it's the truth. We do have to get up, put one foot in front of the other and go about the business of living.

Chapter 4

The Game Plan for Your New Life

This handbook has been designed as a "New Life Plan" of sorts, like a "starting over blueprint". In this handbook you will find tools, resources, and techniques to start your life over and/or give you more "life tools" to help you wherever you are right now. There is a saying in business that goes; "When the only tool you have is hammer – every problem looks like a nail". With this handbook you are being given a "Swiss Army Knife" of various tools for your prosperity.

The proven tools, methods and techniques are being used by some of the most successful people in world. Some of them will admit they are using these tools, and some will not, as to some, they are their "Secret Weapons" of their success. When starting over it is a good time to reexamine the way things are being done in your life and I encourage you to reexamine your life as well. What's working and what's not working? What needs to change? As I used to sell computers many years ago, there was a joke we had amongst the sales people when working with some prospective customers that went like this – *"I want a new computer system that did what my old computer system did even though my old computer system did it wrong (and the other part of this joke was - and make sure it creates this report that no one ever looks at and that we keep it file folder in the filing cabinet that no one ever opens)!* When starting over again you just don't want to replace what you were doing with the same thing, you want to replace it with something even better. A better job or even your business perhaps. A better quality of life. Better relationships. Better health. Better everything!

This handbook is your new "Game Plan" for a better life for you and your family. **Plan, Create and Execute your new game plan, and live a better life than you had before the pandemic.** I did not say it was going to be easy and it's not about being easy or hard. It's about doing better, being better and living a better and more prosperous life than you had before. You, your family, and your friends will appreciate it and are worth it!

PART II:

The Spiritual

(Our Life Force)

NOTES

Chapter 5

New Beginning Quotes

- *"Even the greatest was once a beginner. Don't be afraid to take that first step."*

  - Muhammad Ali

- *"The secret to a rich life is to have more beginnings than endings."*

  - Dave Weinbaum

- "Don't be afraid if things seem difficult in the beginning. That's only the initial impression. The important thing is not to retreat; you have to master yourself."

  - Olga Korbut

- "First comes thought; then organization of that thought, into ideas and plans; then transformation of those plans into reality. The beginning, as you will observe, is in your imagination."

  - Napoleon Hill

- *"The distance is nothing; it's only the first step that is difficult."*

  - Marquise du Deffand

- *"Discontent is the first necessity of progress."*

  - Thomas Edison

- *"Small opportunities are often the beginning of great enterprises."*

  - Demosthenes

- *"We are meant to keep focused for new life, for new beginnings, for new experiences, and to use our abilities to move beyond all those things that may serve as excuses to confine us to the now."*

  - Byron Pulsifer

- *"Making the beginning is one third of the work."*

  - Irish Proverb

- *"A journey of a thousand miles must begin with a single step."*

  - Lao-Tsu

- *"The start of something new brings the hope of something great, ANYTHING IS POSSIBLE."*

  - Author Unknown

- *"The way to get started is to quit talking and begin doing."*

  - Walt Disney

Chapter 6

Why Are We Here on This Beautiful Planet

I would ask that you be a bit open minded. I would ask that you be "open to the possibility of…" I would also ask you to suspend your belief system for a short while and be open to a new way of thinking; this chapter is just one of these areas that I would ask you to do these things.

I would ask you to think about the true meaning of life, the true meaning of *your* life. And though this has been a question that has been pondered and discussed for millennia, it is just as fresh and relative **now** as it was then. The purpose of asking this question is to open one's mind to understand that we as individuals are part of a whole.

What whole is that you ask? The whole of this planet, the whole of all of human kind; even I dare say, the whole of the Universe and in being part of this whole, this means that each one of us has a unique role in this whole. And, that unique role is performing "Our Work" (another way of thinking about "our work" is our Life Purpose) and our work is unique to each of us. Let's go a step further with these concepts.

What if this planet is "a classroom" or "a community" of some type; and in this classroom or community, we are here to learn certain lessons of sorts, maybe even call them "life lessons" and do "our work". What if these life lessons were meant to help us grow as individuals, to become better people, better human beings and help others grow as well? What if this was all true? How would you live your life? What would you do and what would you **not** do?

Whatever your beliefs are, do you think the above is possible? Do you think it applies to all of us? Do you think you would live your life differently? By the time we finish our time together this entire section will have a different perspective for you.

Let's spend a little time exploring some of these questions; the answers will help you find your life's true purpose.

Exercise: Answer these questions to the best of your ability. There are no right or wrong answers. Just ponder these areas and be open to the possibilities. Take as long as you need on this exercise. Write some now, write some later and write again even later still. This exercise will help you to find your true life purpose.

1. What do you think is the meaning of life?
2. What do you think is the meaning of **your** life?
3. Do you think we/you are here on this planet in this time and this place for a specific reason?
4. Do you believe we are part of a whole? Why or why not?

Chapter 7

Being Human – What Does It Really Mean

What does it really mean to be human? We human beings are made up of four components or aspects.

1. The Physical (of the Body)

2. The Mental (of the Mind)

3. The Emotional (of the Heart – the Emotional Heart)

4. The Spiritual (of the Spirit – the Life Force within).

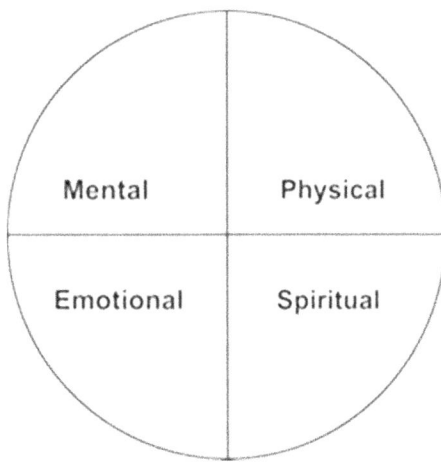

These 4 components are **interdependent** upon one another. What happens to one component has an impact on the other components. Each of the components has a function of its own and together they comprise a human being or the attributes of being human.

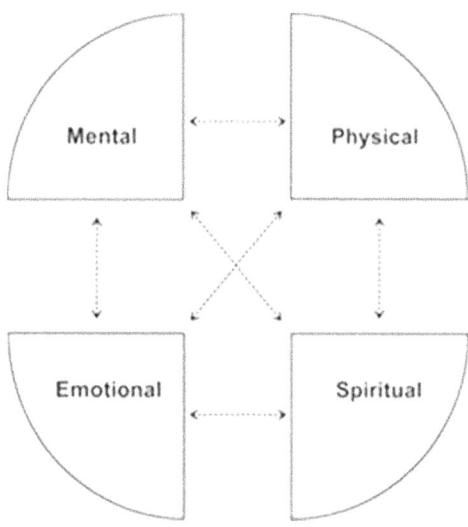

If any of these four components are out of balance we experience **"Dis-ease"**. When we experience "dis-ease" in the Body, it becomes illness/sickness. When in the Mind it becomes mental illness of sorts. In the Heart, it becomes "heart ache" or emotional disorders. In the spiritual, it is viewed as being "spiritually disconnected".

To achieve optimum wellness, each component needs to be kept free from "dis-ease". This is achieved by "exercising" each area.

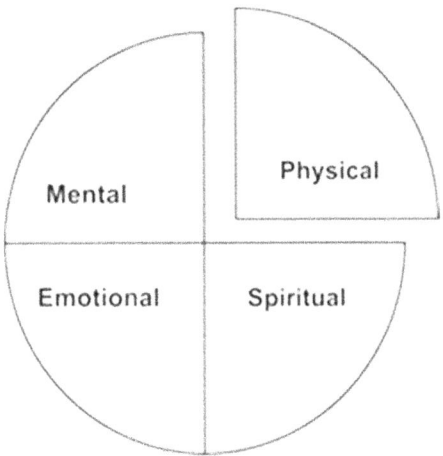

The Physical is exercised through the body by feeding it proper nourishment, performing proper physical activity, and keeping away from anything deemed "poisons" to the body.

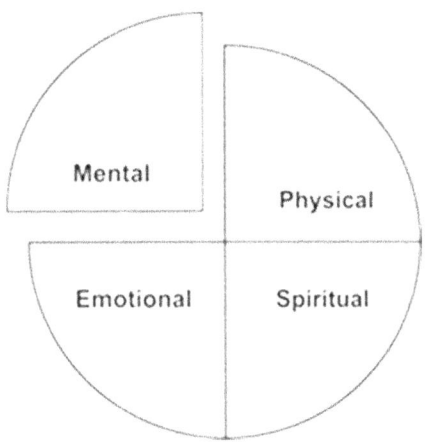

The Mental is exercised by reading, viewing appropriate events, and doing positive visualizations. As the mind works like a computer;, if you put garbage in you will get garbage out.

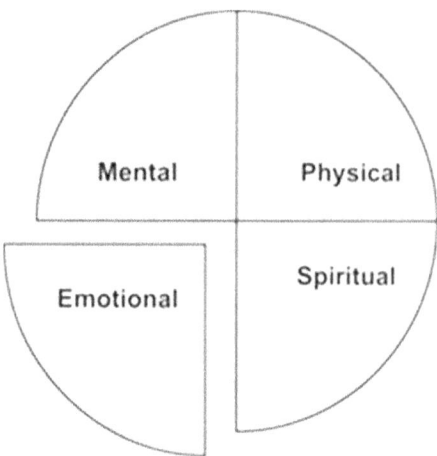

The Emotional is exercised by demonstrating acts of love; for self, for those close to us and all human kind. Performing acts of service.

The Spiritual is exercised by meditation on one's connection to Nature, the Universe, the Source, The Creator, or God.

In seeking your life purpose you will find that all of the above components (physical, mental, emotional, and spiritual) of your life need to be in balance. For what good will it do you when you find your true work and attain the prosperity you desire if you are physically ill, mentally exhausted, emotionally drained, and not connected spiritually to anything. How can you have a fulfilling life if you have any and all "dis-ease" going on?

It is so important to have the proper balance in your life in all the four areas; **Physically** – to eat right and exercise, **Mentally** – to think good thoughts and put good things into one's mind, **Emotionally** – to open one's heart to a healthy love of one's self and to love others and **Spiritually** – to make and keep conscious contact with your Higher Power, whatever that may mean to you, be it God, the Universe, nature, human kind, etc.

As discussed earlier, when we get "out of balance" in any areas of our lives we experience "dis-ease" and this dis-ease can and will affect our work and our life purpose. That is why being in balance and staying in balance is so important. For those of us who have found our 'true work" it is important that we are good examples to help those that are seeking their work and purpose. This does not mean we are to be perfect for we all are human and must deal with the trials and tribulations of being such; however, we should do our best to strive to be in balance to the best of our abilities.

Exercise: Answer these questions to the best of your ability. There are no right or wrong answers. Just ponder these areas and be open to the possibilities.

1. What happens to you when you are out of balance – physically, mentally, emotionally, and spiritually?

2. What can you do to get back into balance – physically, mentally, emotionally, and spiritually?

NOTES

NOTES

Chapter 8

Some Exercises to Make Your Creativity Flow!

The following simple exercises are meant to center you physically, mentally, emotionally, and spiritually. None of these exercises are difficult. You will quickly observe and enjoy the positive benefits of these exercises and techniques. **Although none of the following exercises are strenuous. As with any new exercise program, you are advised to check with your doctor before you begin.**

The main benefit of these exercises is to help your creativity flow as well as having you achieve balance in your life as we spoke about in the previous chapter. When we have balance in our lives everything seems to flow easier, with ease and grace. When we are out of balance, everything becomes much more of a struggle.

It's best to perform these exercises on a daily basis. Just do what feels right. There is no need for stress or strain as there is no need to reach a specific goal. It is always about "progress and not perfection".

Exercise – Breathing for Relaxation

Taking deep **s-l-o-w** breaths in and out will help you relax.

The benefit of this exercise is to help one become calm, peaceful, and centered.

1. Take a slow deep **breath in** for a count up to four – one, two, three, four.

2. Then slowly **exhale out** for a count up to four – one, two, three, four.

3. Take a slow deep **breath in** for a count up to four – one, two, three, four.

4. Then slowly **exhale out** for a count up to four – one, two, three, four.

5. Take a slow **deep breath in** for a count up to four – one, two, three, four.

6. Then slowly **exhale out** for a count up to four – one, two, three, four.

7. Perform this exercise 3 or 4 times and notice how relaxed you become.

You can do this exercise as often as you like.

Exercise – Clear Your Mind

This exercise helps you clear your mind. For example, when you are thinking about too many things or are on "Mind Overload".

The benefit of this exercise is to help you be calm, relaxed and think clearly.

1. Sit comfortably in a quiet environment.
2. Close your eyes and slowly begin to breathe deeply to a count of four
   (1 – 2 – 3 – 4).
3. Mentally focus on the word - **RELAX**.
4. If other thoughts enter your mind, gently bring your attention back to the word – **RELAX**.
5. Calmly, breathe and do it again.
6. Continue for a few minutes.
7. Open your eyes and stretch – inhale and exhale fully.

You can do this exercise as often as you like.

Exercise – Visualization for Your Life Purpose

Visualization (or you may hear the term Guided Imagery) refers to the practice of seeking to affect the outer world by changing one's thoughts. You can choose to visualize anything you desire in life, including your life purpose. You may want to record this exercise and play it back to yourself.

The benefit of this exercise is to help you create an environment that can help you visualize your life purpose.

1. Find a place that is quiet, and you will not be disturbed. Now close your eyes and take a nice deep breath. Take a nice deep, deep breath. Relax your mind; relax your body. You are totally calm and totally relaxed; totally calm and totally relaxed.

2. Count from four down to the number one. With every number you count, I would like you to take a deep breath, and each time say the word "relax," Relax and exhale the breath from your body. With every number you count, take a deep breath, and each time say the word "relax", relax, and allow the breath to exhale from your body.

Four, take a nice deep breath (pause) and relax.

Three, take a nice deep breath (pause) and relax.

Two, take a nice deep, deep breath (pause) and relax.

One, deep breath (pause)... and relax. Relax your thoughts; relax your body.

Very good, now continue to breathe normally.

3. Now count from four down to one again. Mentally release each group of muscles that is called to your attention.

Four, release the muscles in head and face. Just release and relax. Feel your head slowly drop forward if that is comfortable for you.

Three, release the muscles in your neck and shoulders. Just release and relax any stress and any strain.

Two, release the muscles in your back and allow your hands to fall to your sides if you wish.

One, release the muscles in your stomach and feel the relaxation flow down through your legs and feet.

Like a series of dominoes, all the muscles in your body begin at the top of your head and flow into one another as each one releases and relaxes.

With every beat of your heart, with every breath that you take, you will become more relaxed, calmer, more relaxed, calmer…

… Good. Continue to use your imagination. Imagine the warm, golden sun going down into your skin and melting deeply within every cell of your body.

4. The gentle warmth flows over through your muscles, allowing them to relax. Release and relax all of the tension; all of the strain.

Feel the muscles in your neck and shoulders expand.

Notice how you feel - without stress - free in your body and mind. Your heart rate and breathing are calm and relaxed. Your muscles are totally relaxed. Totally calm, totally relaxed. Totally calm, totally relaxed.

5. Now, think about a time in the **future**. In a vision, see yourself living your life's purpose. What type of work are you doing? Where are you doing it? With what type of people? Are there any specific smells? Use all of your senses. See it. Touch it. Experience it! Just let it come to you…

6. See yourself living your life's purpose. Being happy, fulfilled, prosperous, you are full of joy and wonderment. So happy doing your work!

7. When I count to four... you will be wide awake...feeling good and alert. Remembering everything you experienced in your visualization and able to write it down if you wish....One...you're beginning to come back...Two... feel the energy start flowing through your body...Three… moving your fingers and toes... more and more awake...feel the energy running through your body ...Four... breathing in wakeful energy... clearing your head... balancing your energies... feeling wonderful in every way..., opening your eyes... fully coming back... fully back... wide awake... and ready to go...

You can do this exercise once a day.
You can do it more if you like.

Exercise – Connecting with Nature

Connecting with nature is an excellent way to feel connected to the planet; to Mother Earth, to feel grounded and calm.

The benefit of this exercise is to understand nature and how important nature and all the plants and animals are in our lives.

1. Grow a Plant – If you cannot go to nature then bring nature to you by growing a plant. You don't need a lot of space and you can observe nature up close and personal.

2. Hug a Tree – Want to feel nature? Next time you see a tree go give it a nice big hug! Yes, that may seem a little corny, but trees do help us everyday.

3. Go to a Park – The park is always a good place to go to be with nature. Touch the grass, see the animals, hear the birds, smell the flowers, or taste the water (just make sure that the water is clean ☺).

4. Go to the Ocean, a Lake, a Stream or Pond – Visit a body of water and observe the fish and wildlife that live there.

5. Go to the Mountains – Connect with nature on a mountain. Take in the fresh, clean, crisp mountain air. Go for a hike with friends or join a club.

6. Go to the Local Animal Shelter – Visit with a friend or by yourself, a local animal shelter and connect to the animals there. Animals need attention and love too!

7. Go to the Zoo – If you really want to connect with nature, go to a zoo and see all the different animals there. You will learn so much from the different animals from around the world.

You can do these exercises as often as your time and schedule permit. Try to do it at least once a week.

Exercise – Yoga

Yoga is a series of postures and breathing exercises practiced achieving control of the body, mind and spirit to help achieve tranquility and peace of mind.

The benefit of these exercises is to attain control over your body and mind and to achieve a sense of well-being.

Before doing any new and different exercises, check with your doctor.

Fifteen Minute Yoga Practice

Perform each pose for up to 6 breathes.

Tree Pose (Tadasana)

The Tree Pose helps strengthen your thighs, calves, ankles and back. It can also increase the flexibility of your hips and groin. Your balance and concentration can also be improved with constant practice. This Yoga Pose is recommended for people who have sciatica and flat feet.

Triangle Pose (Trikonasana)

In Hindu art, the triangle is a potent symbol for the divine principle, and it is frequently found in the yantras and mandalas used for meditation. The Trikonasana or Triangle Pose concludes the Yoga Postures in our basic session.

Warrior Pose

The Warrior Pose stretches and strengthens the arms and legs, increases stamina, improve balance and concentration, and can also relieve backaches. If you are suffering from diarrhea, high blood pressure or neck problems, you should take extra caution practicing this pose.

Dog Pose (Adho Mukha Shvanasana)

The Dog Pose improves flexibility of your spine, stretches the hips and middle and low back, rejuvenates the body, and helps in preventing back problems. Take note that this Yoga Pose should not be performed if you have serious back pain or injury.

Double Leg Raises

A Double Leg Raise is similar to a Single Leg Raise, only this time, you will raise both legs. In doing this Yoga Pose, make sure that the full length of your back is resting on the floor and your shoulders and neck are relaxed. This section covers the steps and guidelines on how to do this pose properly.

Yoga Exercise - Final Corpse

For you to appreciate the benefits of relaxation, you should first be familiar on how it is to be tense. This is what happens when you do the Final Corpse. Everything related to that position including suggestions on how to do it is discussed in further detail in this article.

Source: http://www.abc-of-yoga.com

NOTES

Exercise – Physical Exercise

Physical activity will contribute to our growth process. Physical exercise can improve the cardiovascular functions and contributes to a healthy skeletal muscle system.

Physical exercise and a well-balanced diet will help to regulate weight and can prevent obesity.

The benefits of this exercise are many; to release excess energy, staying in shape; relaxing the body and the mind, also assists in calming the mind and spirit.

Before doing any new and different exercises, check with your doctor.

1. Stretching - Stretching exercises are used to prevent injury and prepare your body for exercising all the body muscles. **Stretching** is a powerful part of any exercise program. **Stretching** works in conjunction with muscles to improve athletic performance, joint flexibility and maintain good body posture. Stretching warms up the muscles.

2. Walking - Walking is not only a great exercise for maintaining health; it's also one of the best exercises to help control weight. There are many benefits to be gained from walking. These can include more energy, deeper and more satisfying sleep, stronger leg muscles, less knee pounding than running, lower body fat, higher metabolic rate and reducing stress. Many students, who walk or exercise, study more effectively and have better recall.

3. Jogging - Jogging is one of the simplest exercise programs, as it produces many benefits. You can do it by yourself. It helps you build a good physique by stimulating your heart rate, relieving stress, and toning your muscles. It increases your energy level and it brings a sense of discipline; it is more result oriented than any other type of workout. It also helps burn calories and helps you stay fit.

4.Networking Events with Others – Attending networking events with others, though a simple concept, produces many benefits including and not limited to, meeting new people, and interaction and socialization with others and making new contacts that can help you with your life purpose.

5. Yoga - As previously mentioned, Yoga exercises help us to attain body and mental control and achieve a sense of well-being.

6. Martial Arts - The benefits of Martial Arts are many; they teach physical and mental strength training, discipline, leadership skills and how to interact with others. The martial arts have many different styles, offensive and defensive techniques. Both are effective in their benefits to us.

7. Play Team Sports – Regardless of the sport, playing team sports with others in a team environment helps us get along with other people to achieve a common goal. Working together, they are all winners.

You can do these exercises as often as your time and schedule permit.

NOTES

Chapter 9

A Little Bit of Spiritual Stuff to Help You on Your Journey

Spirituality offers many benefits to our lives. Developing your spiritual life can give you a sense of purpose. People who have taken time to develop their spiritual life are likely to better understand their needs, wants and desires.

It's unfortunate that there is so much misconception about spirituality. Spirituality is not religion. One may be spiritual and not religious. One may be religious and not spiritual. As well as being neither religious nor spiritual. It is not the purpose of this book to discuss the merits of religion, as the work discussed here is meant to be "in addition to and not instead of" your current religious and/or spiritual practices.

We are all spiritual beings. Other than our physical appearance, what makes the YOU in YOU? Out of all the billions of people on this planet it is your spirit that makes you unique. The exercises in this section are meant to help you connect with the spiritual side of your being. As we have spoken before, there is a spiritual component of our being. If you re-call, we mentioned that we humans are made up of the following four components – the spiritual, the emotional, the mental, and the physical.

Here are two exercises that will help you connect with your spirituality. These two exercises are **Prayer and Mediation**. It is said that if you want to speak to God (or your Higher Power, the Universe, Nature, or whatever you believe in) you Pray and if you want to hear the answer to those prayers you Meditate.

As for Prayer, there is no right way or wrong way to pray. The main thing is to quiet yourself and speak what's in your heart and in your mind. There are countless books on the subject of prayer that will be of help. The main thing to be mindful when praying is to think you are speaking with a friend, a very close and dear friend, and the rest will all come out easily and naturally. What should you pray about? Whatever your needs, wants and desire are, or for those people that you would like to help, or for the planet, the list is endless. A suggestion is pray for guidance as to find your life purpose and your work. It's a good place to start.

Meditation is an excellent tool to align body, mind, and spirit. Meditation helps quiet your mind of all the chatter of our lives, the chatter of the outside world in our heads, and the chatter in the inside of our heads. Want to know your life purpose and work? Meditate on it. You are sure to get answers that will help you on your journey!

Feeling stressed, anxious, not sure of things. Meditate. You will achieve a sense of calmness and serenity. When we are calm and serene, we can handle anything that comes our way. Start meditating 5 minutes in the morning and 5 minutes in the evening (or anytime you like). You will notice significant changes in your life within 30 days or less. You'll be able to handle whatever comes your way in calm, level-headed and serene manner.

If you want proof that mediation works, take a piece of paper, and **write how you feel right now** and really tell the truth as only you will be reading it. Then meditate and do the exercise again and compare the difference, you will be pleasantly surprised.

While there are many types and forms of meditation, here is a simple meditation that you can do anytime **(not while driving a car or using heavy machinery, etc.)**, any place without any equipment. This meditation technique is extremely helpful for people that have difficulty quieting their minds.

Exercise – Meditation

Meditation is aligning **Mind, Body, Emotions and Spirit**, so that these components function as one. Meditating is the practice of quieting the mind of all its chatter to enable you to be open to the thoughts of the Universe.

The benefit of this exercise is to become centered in one's self.

1. This is the "**1 – 2 – 3 – 4**" **Method of Meditation**.

2. Take a slow deep **breath in** for a count up to four – one, two, three, four.

3. Then slowly **exhale out** for a count up to four – one, two, three, four.

4. Take a total of 3 or 4 slow deep breaths.

5. Then just say to yourself, in your mind, "**1 – 2 – 3 – 4**" over and over again.

6. The purpose of this is to focus your mind on the counting and away from the chatter that is with us in our mind.

7. There is no right way or wrong way to perform this meditation. Do what you feel is comfortable and natural for you. There is no need for stress or strain. In time you will have no need for counting "**1 – 2 – 3 – 4**". You will be

able to close your eyes and go into a calm, relaxing and peaceful meditative state.

You can do this exercise in the morning before you start your day for 5 minutes and when you end your day for 5 minutes.

NOTES

Chapter 10

Spiritual Guidance: Finding Your Purpose from Some Interesting Sources

As previously mentioned, I would ask you to be open to new thoughts, experiences, and new ways of thinking. What if we were not on this journey called life alone? What if we had "Spiritual Helpers" with us on our journey? What if we can get guidance about our life purpose and work with our unseen helpers? At first glance I know this may seem like a lot to take in, however, most if not all of the religious and spiritual traditions have these spiritual helpers. Let's spend some time discussing these helpers and how they can benefit you with your life purpose and your work.

We will be discussing Angels, Spirit Guides and Ascended Masters and what each is and their unique purpose in our lives. They help make up our "Spiritual Team".

Angels – Angels are messengers. If we will just open our minds and hearts to the possibility that angels exist and ask for their assistance, they will inspire us, help us create health and abundance, and live in peace and harmony. They radiate unconditional love and will help us do the same. However, we must ask for their assistance as we have "free will" and they will not infringe on your will without our permission.

Spirit Guides - The term Spirit Guide generally makes reference to one or more entities who watch, teach, heal, and help us on our physical journey into spiritual awareness. They are above in higher frequency, while we experience the physical below. A spirit guide is there simply *to **guide***, not as an entity that you need to give yourself over to in any manner.

Ascended Masters – Ascended Masters are spiritually enlightened beings who in past incarnations were ordinary humans, but who have undergone a process of spiritual transformation.

There are six ways that your "spiritual team" can and will give you inspiration and guidance for your life purpose. These ways are called the "Six Clairs". They are:

1. Clairvoyance (vision/seeing) - The faculty of perceiving things or events in the future or beyond normal sensory contact.

2. Clairsentience (feeling/touching) - Is the ability to feel and experience the energy in an intuitive way.

3. Clairaudience (hearing/listening) - The faculty of perceiving, as if by hearing, what is inaudible.

4. Clairalience (smelling) - The ability for a person to acquire psychic knowledge by means of smelling.

5. Claircognizance (knowing) – The ability to know things without much effort.

6. Clairgustance (tasting) - The ability to taste a substance without putting anything in one's mouth.

This all may be new and make you feel somewhat uneasy. But imagine the possibilities of your own dedicated "Spiritual Team" helping you, working with you to help you with your life purpose and anything else. These beings are dedicated to our happiness, health, and wellbeing. What if it were all true? Read books and articles about your "spiritual team" and ask them to help you with your life purpose. You'll be glad you did. Ask and then start noticing all the coincidences and synchronicities that happen. There will be too many to explain away. Try it! What have you got to lose?

Exercise: Spend some quiet time with your "Spiritual Team", (one at a time) and start asking for help with your life purpose. Keep a journal and write down any and all inspirations that you receive in any form you receive them (remember the "Six Clairs") to validate your conversations. Every time you spend some quiet time with your spiritual team update your journal. Observe over a period of time any messages, information, patterns, etc. that you are receiving, especially if you are focusing on one particular issue (Ex.: Direction with your life purpose).

NOTES

Chapter 11

Prosperity: What is the True Meaning?

What is Prosperity? Webster's dictionary defines prosperity as, "the condition of being successful or thriving; especially economic well-being". Defining Prosperity really depends with whom you are talking to about this subject. To some people it means money, wealth, and financial success. To others, it's health, peace of mind, love, friends, and family. **Prosperity means whatever <u>YOU</u> want it to mean!** There is no right or wrong answer. I am certain there are as many different expressions of prosperity as there are people on the planet.

How do we invoke Prosperity? How do we make it come to us, into our lives? There are various methods to bringing prosperity into our lives. You will learn some practical exercises to achieve a rich, happy, and joyous life!

Exercise:

1. What does prosperity mean to you?

2. What do you need to be prosperous? – clearing define with specific examples

3. How can you help others to be prosperous?

NOTES

Chapter 12

You Have the Power to Create Your Perfect Life Experience

The famous American self-help author Oliver "Napoleon Hill" known best for his book ***Think and Grow Rich*** (1937) which is among the 10 bestselling self-help books of all time. **Hill's** works insisted that fervid expectations are essential to improving one's life. One of his famous quotes was – *"Whatever the mind of man/woman can conceive and believe, it can achieve."* With that said below are some exercises to help you conceive a new and better life, so you can believe it and then achieve it.!

Visualization

Having mentioned this exercise in a previous chapter I want to bring it to your attention again in conjunction with other similar exercises. Visualization (or Creative Visualization which is the same as Guided Imagery) refers to the practice of seeking to affect the outer world by changing one's thoughts. You can choose to visualize anything you desire in life, including your life purpose. You may want to record this exercise and play it back to yourself. Use visualization to see in your mind's eye the type of prosperity you are seeking.

Exercise – Visualization for Your Prosperity

The benefit of this exercise is to help you create an environment that can help you visualize prosperity.

1. Find a place that is quiet, and you will not be disturbed. Now close your eyes and take a nice deep breath. Take a nice deep, deep breath. Relax your mind; relax your body. You are totally calm and totally relaxed; totally calm and totally relaxed.

2. Count from four down to the number one. With every number you count, I would like you to take a deep breath, and each time say the word "relax,." Relax and exhale the breath from your body. With every number you count, take a deep breath, and each time say the word "relax",; relax and allow the breath to exhale from your body.

Four, take a nice deep breath (pause) and relax.

Three, take a nice deep breath (pause) and relax.

Two, take a nice deep, deep breath (pause) and relax.

One, deep breath (pause)... and relax. Relax your thoughts; relax your body.

Very good, now continue to breathe normally.

3. Now count from four down to one again. Mentally release each group of muscles that is called to your attention.

Four, release the muscles in the head and face. Just release and relax. Feel your head slowly drop forward if that is comfortable for you.

Three, release the muscles in your neck and shoulders. Just release and relax any stress and any strain.

Two, release the muscles in your back and allow your hands to fall to your sides if you wish.

One, release the muscles in your stomach and feel the relaxation flow down through your legs and feet.

Like a series of dominoes, all the muscles in your body begin at the top of your head and flow into one another as each one releases and relaxes.

With every beat of your heart, with every breath that you take, you will become more relaxed, calmer, more relaxed, calmer...

... Good. Continue to use your imagination. Imagine the warm, golden sun going down into your skin and melting deeply within every cell of your body.

4. The gentle warmth flows over through your muscles, allowing them to relax. Release and relax all of the tension; all of the strain.

Feel the muscles in your neck and shoulders expand.

Notice how you feel - without stress - free in your body and mind. Your heart rate and breathing are calm and relaxed. Your muscles are totally relaxed. Totally calm, totally relaxed. Totally calm, totally relaxed.

5. Now, think about a time in the not too distant **future**. In a vision, see yourself living the life you want to lead. A life full of prosperity, whatever prosperity means to you, and enjoying the lifestyle you want to lead. It could be a life filled with lots of money, good health, loved ones, friends, whatever you want it to mean.

What type working are you doing? Where are you doing it and with what type of people? Use all of your senses. Are there any specific smells? See it. Touch it. Experience it! Just let it come to you...

6. See yourself being prosperous. Being happy, fulfilled, you are full of joy and wonderment. So happy to be prosperous and living the lifestyle you choose!

LONG PAUSE...

7. When I count to four... you will slowly awake...feeling good and alert. Remembering everything you experienced in your visualization and able to write it down if you wish....One...you're beginning to come back...Two... feel the energy start flowing through your body...Three... moving your fingers and toes... more and more awake...feel the energy running through your body ...Four... breathing in wakeful energy... clearing your head... balancing your energies... feeling wonderful in every way..., opening your eyes... fully coming back... fully back... wide awake... and ready to go...

You can do this exercise once a day.
You can do it more if you like.

Brainstorming

Brainstorming is a group or individual creativity technique by which efforts are made to find a conclusion for a specific problem by gathering a list of ideas spontaneously contributed by its member(s). There is also brainstorming software. Google the words "Brainstorming" and "Mind Mapping Software" for more information. The software, much of it free, will be a very helpful to guide you visually to what you would like to accomplish with your business.

Below is a sample of the product I use called **SimpleMind** (http://www.simpleapps.eu/simplemind/). I use it on my computer, tablet and mobile phone to brainstorm new ideas, projects and concepts I'm working on.

Example of brainstorming using mind mapping software:

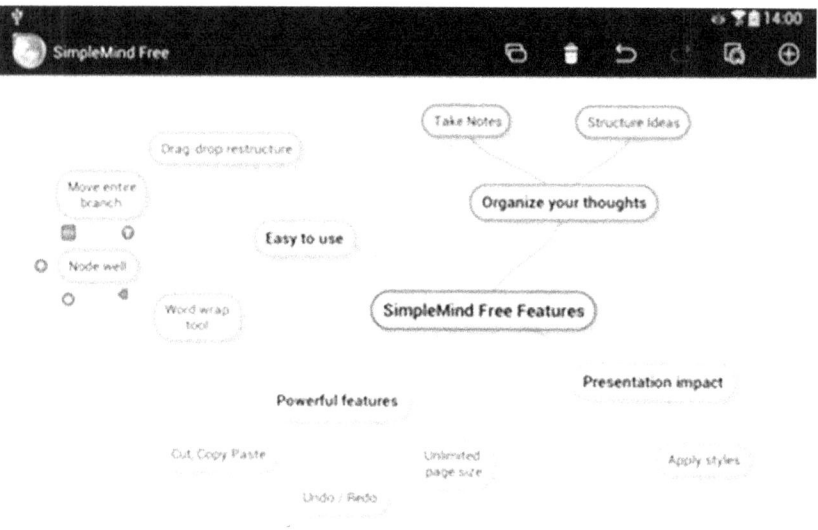

Vision Boards

A Vision Board is a large piece of paperboard to post images to depict goals and dreams in all areas of your life, or in just one specific area that you are focusing on, which inspire you and make you feel good. It helps keep you focused on your goal(s).

An Example Vision Board:

NOTES

PART III:

The Emotional

(Our Emotional Heart)

NOTES

Chapter 13

More New Beginning Quotes

- "Beginning today, treat everyone you meet as if they were going to be dead by midnight. Extend to them all the care, kindness, and understanding you can muster, and do it with no thought of any reward. Your life will never be the same again."

    - Og Mandino

- "One paints the beginning of a certain end. The other, the end of a sure beginning."

    - Maya Angelou

- "When faced with a large project, remember you move a mountain one stone at a time."

    - Catherine Pulsifer

- "New beginnings are exciting! They become exciting to us because they offer the promise of hope, the anticipation of change in our lives, and the prospect that our dreams will indeed come true!"

    - Squire Rushnell

- "Let your first success be just a beginning. Let your dreams chase you."

    - Amit Ahlawat

- "As you begin to live a more positive life, it simply makes sense that you take a look at your dreams and goals to see if you are living in a way that will best allow you to accomplish them."

    - Chris Johnston

- "There will come a time when you believe everything is finished. That will be the beginning."

    - Louis L'Amour

- "The bad news is that most people give up; they settle for second best; they don't start over; they stay stuck. Please don't allow that to be you."

    - Doug Fields

- "You need to learn from your mistakes to start a new beginning because if you stop then you will not able to accomplish your goals in life."

    - Ivan Hakin

- "No one can ever take your memories from you - each day is a new beginning, make good memories every day."

    - Catherine Pulsifer

- "What we call the beginning is often the end. And to make an end is to make a beginning. The end is where we start from."

    - T.S. Eliot

Chapter 14

Emotional Baggage – The Personal Clutter that Hold You Back

In this section we will be discussing the "Emotional" aspect of being human and how important it is to your wellbeing in all aspects of your life. While the work in this section in particular and the entire handbook is not meant to take the place of working with mental health or other specific professionals, it will help you on your path to a better life. The exercises in this handbook should be viewed as tools to be used "in addition to and not instead of" working with licensed mental health professionals. Should you feel you require professional help it is advised you seek a licensed mental health professional to help you on your journey to emotional wellness.

Emotional baggage can and will hold you back from becoming the true person you are meant to be and reaching your goals in both your professional and personal life. When we have not resolved emotional matters they tend to stay with us until they are resolved. We stuff these emotional matters away in our sub-conscious until we cannot stuff them away any longer until one day they start to spill out of us.

What is Emotional Baggage? What's the impact of emotional baggage in your life? What can be done to get rid of your emotional baggage? Emotional Baggage can be defined as the unresolved emotional issues, traumas, and extremely high stressful events from your past (and sometimes present) that currently weigh heavy on your mind, sub-conscious mind and sometimes even impacting your body. [2]

What's the impact of emotional baggage in your life? One study [3] found that emotional baggage can be a real barrier to making healthy lifestyle changes (like exercising more [4], eating healthier or quitting smoking). "Participants described being burdened by emotional baggage with problems from childhood and/or with family, work and social life issues," found the study. "Respondents said that they felt that emotional baggage was an important explanation for why they were stuck in old habits [5] and that conversely, being stuck in old habits added load to their already emotional baggage and made it heavier."

This baggage can also "interfere with professional ambition or goals [6], healthy relationships, personal contentment and the enjoyment of life," says Karol Ward, LCSW, author of "*Worried Sick: Break Free From Chronic Worry to Achieve Mental and Physical Health.*" "Until you bring to your awareness why your life is not going the way you want; you can feel like a victim, someone who is being tossed around by life's circumstances."

What can be done to get rid of your emotional baggage? Getting rid of emotional baggage is a process and like any process it takes time. How much time depends on how much emotional baggage you have and how much time you are willing to invest in yourself. Having gone through this myself and still going through this, to a lesser degree, I can assure you it will take what it takes to get rid of your emotional baggage, but the rewards are well worth it. As the saying goes "it's an inside job" as the emotional baggage is on the inside, so too the work that needs to be done, is work in ourselves for ourselves.

Having written a book on my personal emotional journey dealing with my own emotional baggage, *"Healing the Holes in My Soul! How I Saved My Own Life, Became Whole to Lead a Happy, Fulfilling and Joyous Life!"* (available on Amazon.com) I am going to share with you the exercises I did to get rid of much of my emotional baggage especially what I call the "big boulders" that have been holding me back to greater prosperity in both my professional and personal life.

Kindly be advised that as I have mentioned in my credentials that I am a Inter-Faith (All Faiths Minister) that many of the exercises mentioned below are faith based self-help exercises that may or may not be in alignment with your personal belief system. These exercises are meant to be an aide on your professional and personal journey and should be used "in addition to and not instead of" working with trained mental health professionals.

Exercises from the book *"Healing the Holes in My Soul! How I Saved My Own Life, Became Whole to Lead a Happy, Fulfilling and Joyous Life!"*:

- **EXERCISE 01:** BEING MAD AT MY PARENTS - TELL <u>EACH</u> PARENT (and/or CAREGIVER) WHY YOU ARE MAD AT THEM AND GIVE THE REASON(S) WHY YOU ARE MAD AT THEM. Take a piece of paper(s) and tell <u>each</u> Parent (and/or Caregiver) the reason(s) why you are mad at them. When you're done, go outside, in a safe place, in a fireproof container and take your letter to them and burn it. The purpose of the exercise is to get the "mad" out of you and place it into the paper and then burn the paper, so the "mad" feelings are out of your system (psyche) and sent into the air so they don't come back to bother you any longer. Do this exercise as many times as necessary (Does not have to be in one sitting. Can be over a period of time) until all of the "mad" is out of you. Fire is a very important basic element, that helps to transmute (change in form, nature, or substance) things. Fire needs to be respected when working with it. Remember always being safe when working with fire.

- **EXERCISE 02:** BEING MAD AT GOD - TELL GOD YOU ARE MAD AT GOD AND GIVE THE REASON(S) WHY YOU ARE MAD AT GOD. Take a piece of paper(s) and tell God the reason(s) why you are mad at God. Yes, this exercise is the same as the one in Chapter 1, but this one is about being mad at God. When you're done, go outside, in a safe place, in a fireproof container and take your letter to God and burn it. The purpose of the exercise is to get the "mad" out of you and place it into the paper and then burn the paper, so the "mad" reasons are out of your system (psyche) and sent into the air so they don't come back to bother you any longer. Fire is a very important basic element, that helps to transmute (change in form, nature, or substance) things and needs to be respected when working with it. Remember always be safe when working with fire.

- **EXERCISE 03:** JOURNALING - BUY YOURSELF A NOTEBOOK WITH LINED PAPER AND START WRITING DOWN WHATEVER COMES UP. Start getting into the habit of writing and you will be surprised what "bubbles up". You will start seeing in your writings, what you need to deal with that has been suppressed, repressed and any painful feelings. These feelings, emotions, events, etc. is the "work" that you have to do, process and heal yourself from. There are professionals to help you with the work (your work), self-help groups and books, but ultimately you still must do the work yourself. You don't have to go it alone. There are some resources in the back of this book to give you some suggestions.

- **EXERCISE 04:** IDENTIFYING YOUR EMOTIONAL PAIN. In your notebook start to write down all of your "Emotional Pain". This is your personal notebook, and nobody needs to see it. Go to a quiet place and center yourself. Pray and meditation is very helpful. Being in nature is also very helpful. Write the emotional pain that you carry so it can be processed and released from your soul. Start getting into the habit of writing and you will be surprised what "bubbles up". You will start seeing in your writings what you need to deal with that has been suppressed, repressed and any painful feelings. These feelings, emotions, events, etc. is the "work" that you have to do, to process and heal yourself. There are professionals to help you with the work (your work), self-help groups and books, but ultimately you still must do the work yourself. You don't have to go it alone. There are resources towards the end of the book to give you some suggestions.

- **EXERCISE 05:** BEING ALONE – GET INVOLVED WITH SOMETHING MEANINGFUL. We don't need to be alone if we do not choose to. Get involve with something meaningful in your life. Be it a local food pantry, animal rescue or whatever resonates with you. You will find that by helping others that need help, you will no longer be alone, be meeting new people and have new life experiences. By helping others, we are always helping ourselves. A good place to start is online by going to websites like www.MeetUp.com, Facebook (and other social media websites) or just go to your favorite search engine and typing the words "Local Groups Near Me."

- **EXERCISE 06**: FIND YOUR SPIRITUAL PATH OR CREATE YOUR OWN PERSONAL PATH TO GOD.

- **EXERCISE 07**: THIS IS A TWO-PART EXERCISE. <u>PART ONE</u>: DO YOU HAVE PAIN, ANGER AND SORROW IN YOUR LIFE? IF SO, DESCRIBE IN DETAIL WHAT IT IS. DO PART ONE OVER AND OVER AGAIN UNTIL YOU CANNOT WRITE ANY MORE ABOUT THE TOPIC MENTIONED. <u>PART TWO</u>: WHAT CAN YOU DO TO HELP YOU BE HAPPY?

- **EXERCISE 08**: HAVE YOU EXPERIENCE 'THE DARKNESS' IN YOUR LIFE? IF SO, DESCRIBE IT IN DETAIL AND WRITE ABOUT IT OVER AND OVER AGAIN UNTIL YOU CANNOT WRITE ANY MORE ABOUT IT.

- **EXERCISE 09**: DO YOU FEEL DEPRESSED NOW OR HAVE BEEN DEPRESSED FOR ANY PERIOD OF TIME? IF SO, DESCRIBE IT IN DETAIL AND WRITE ABOUT IT OVER AND OVER AGAIN UNTIL YOU CANNOT WRITE ANY MORE ABOUT IT.

- **EXERCISE 10:** HAVE YOU EVER EXPERIENCE RAGE? DO YOU CONTINUE TO EXPERIENCE RAGE? IF SO, DESCRIBE IT IN DETAIL AND WRITE ABOUT IT OVER AND OVER AGAIN UNTIL YOU CANNOT WRITE ANY MORE ABOUT IT.

- **EXERCISE 11:** HAVE YOU EVER BEEN ASHAMED OR FEEL ASHAMED NOW? IF SO, DESCRIBE IT IN DETAIL AND WRITE ABOUT IT OVER AND OVER AGAIN UNTIL YOU CANNOT WRITE ANY MORE ABOUT IT.

- **EXERCISE 12:** DO YOU THINK YOU HAVE ADDICTION(S)? IF SO, DESCRIBE THEM IN DETAIL.

- **EXERCISE 13:** DO YOU THINK YOU ARE THE REAL YOU OR ARE YOU FOOLING YOURSELF? DO YOU THINK YOU ARE FOOLING OTHER PEOPLE AS WELL? WRITE ABOUT YOUR THOUGHTS ON THESE SUBJECTS.

- **EXERCISE 14:** HAVE SUICIDAL THOUGHTS BEEN WITH YOU FOR A WHILE? IF SO, WRITE ABOUT THEM HERE.

- **EXERCISE 15:** ANY ISSUES IN YOUR CHILDHOOD AND/OR ADULTHOOD THAT YOU FEEL ARE NOT RESOLVED IN YOUR LIFE? IF SO, WRITE ABOUT THEM HERE.

- **EXERCISE 16:** DO YOU FEEL "DAMAGED" OR "BROKEN"? IF SO, WRITE ABOUT IT HERE.

- **EXERCISE 17:** DO YOU FEEL "CHAINS OF PAIN" IN YOUR FAMILY? IF SO, WRITE ABOUT IT HERE.

- **EXERCISE 18:** DO YOU FEEL YOU HAVE ANY "HOLES IN YOUR SOUL"? IF SO, WRITE ABOUT IT HERE.

- **EXERCISE 19:** DO YOU THINK YOU HAVE AREAS IN YOUR LIFE (PHYSICALLY, MENTALLY, EMOTIONALLY, SPIRITUALLY) THAT NEED TO BE HEALED? IF SO, WRITE ABOUT IT HERE.

- **EXERCISE 20:** ARE THERE ANY PERSON(S) YOU NEED TO FORGIVE? DO YOU NEED TO FORGIVE YOURSELF FOR ANYTHING? IF SO, WRITE ABOUT IT HERE.

- **EXERCISE 21:** DO YOU LOVE YOURSELF? WHY OR WHY NOT? DO YOU LOVE OTHERS? WHY OR WHY NOT? WRITE OUT YOUR THOUGHTS ABOUT THESE SUBJECTS.

- **EXERCISE 22:** DO YOU OWN A PET OR ANIMALS? IF NOT, SPEND SOME TIME A LOCAL ANIMAL SHELTER OR ANIMAL SANCTUARY. WRITE ABOUT YOUR EXPERIENCE AND HOW THE ANIMALS MADE YOU FEEL.

- **EXERCISE 23:** GO SPEND TIME IN NATURE. START BY TURNING EVERYTHING ELECTRONIC OFF FOR 5 MINUTES, THEN 10 MINUTES AND SO ON. WRITE ABOUT YOUR EXPERIENCE.

- **EXERCISE 24:** WHAT ARE YOU GRATEFUL FOR IN YOUR LIFE? WRITE YOUR THOUGHTS ABOUT GRATITUDE. WRITE AND WRITE SOME MORE. DO THIS EXERCISE SEVERAL TIMES UNTIL YOU FEEL GRATITUDE IN YOUR LIFE.

- **EXERCISE 25:** ASK GOD FOR HELP IF YOU ARE FEELING SUICIDAL THEN CONTACT YOUR DOCTOR AND/OR MENTAL HEALTH CARE PROFESSIONAL AND/OR CALL THE SUICIDE HOTLINE. IF YOU'RE NOT FEELING SUICIDAL WRITE A LETTER HELPING SOMEONE WHO IS AND MAIL IT TO THE SUICIDE PREVENTION HOT LINE AND ASK THAT IT BE FORWARDED TO SOMEONE THAT NEEDS HELP.

- **EXERCISE 26:** WHAT'S YOUR LIFE'S PURPOSE? IF YOU KNOW, THEN WRITE WHAT IT IS AND WHAT YOU ENJOY ABOUT YOUR LIFE'S PURPOSE. IF YOU DON'T KNOW YOUR LIFE PURPOSE YET, THEN FIND A BOOK OR TWO ON THE SUBJECT TO HELP YOU FIND YOUR TRUE LIFE'S PURPOSE.

- **EXERCISE 27:** WHAT'S YOUR STORY OF COURAGE? WRITE IT DOWN HERE.

- **EXERCISE 28:** WRITE YOUR OWN PERSONAL PRAYER TO GOD. WRITE IT DOWN HERE.

Chapter 15

Public Service - Service to Others

Many people feel the need and desire to help others. A good way to do this is through public service. Public service can be helping others in a myriad of different ways. By being of service to the public you may be working with people directly in a one-on-one manner, in groups and/or helping mankind in its entirety. In working "one-on-one" with an individual you may be mentoring a young person about a career choice. In a group it might be by working with senior citizens to teach them how to use computers for the first time. A scientist may be helping mankind by developing a vaccine that cures people of an illness. That scientist may never see the people they are helping; however, their work is a public service, nonetheless.

By Helping Others You are Helping Yourself

By helping others, you are in turn helping yourself. There are many benefits of helping others; some benefits are visible while others may not be, however are just as important. By helping others, you are growing your "sphere of influence" meeting new people, establishing contacts which from a business point-of-view may lead to more financial prosperity coming your way. On an emotional level helping others brings tremendous personal satisfaction. You, yes you, can and do make a difference in someone else's life. Your selfless acts quite possibly may be positively changing the course of someone else's life, by improving people lives, making their lives better, and making their lives worth living. By doing your "work" (life purpose) by helping others you will help people find their "work". There is no greater gift to give to others than the gift of doing one's "work" while we are here in this time, in this place, and for you to be the person who showed them to use their own special gifts.

How do I Go About Helping Others?

Helping others does not have to be an elaborate production. It can be as simple as going to your local food pantry, hospital, religious group, town hall, etc. and asking the question, "How can I help?" All helping is honorable and worthy. You may want to make an assessment of your skills and help others with your specific skills. For example, if you know how to set up computers you may want to donate your time to a local charity and set up their computer system. If you are blessed with financial prosperity you may want to make a donation to a worthy cause or organization. There are so many different ways you can help others and be of service. You choose the method that is right for you and watch your life change for the better; see the prosperity start flowing!

You are truly prosperous when you help others. As you help others you are sharing your prosperity, and when you share your prosperity it will come back to you many, many times over.

Below are some resources where you can be of service in helping others. This list is by no means complete and can be used as a starting point for your search:

1. **Volunteer Match** - www.volunteermatch.org

2. **ServiceLeader.org** - www.serviceleader.org/new/virtual/

3. **Extra Hands for ALS** - www.extrahands.org/

4. **Charity Focus -** my.charityfocus.org/login/

5. **Network for Good** - www.networkforgood.org/

6. **Big Brothers Big Sisters** - www.bbbsa.org/

7. **Red Cross** - http://www.redcross.org/

8. **Angel Wish – Help Children Living With HIV-AIDS** - www.angelwish.org/

EXERCISE: In the exercise below, make a listing of all your skills then think about who might be able to use them or benefit from them.

1. What are My Skills (Professional and Personal)

2. Who Needs My Skills (Non-profit organizations, religious groups, etc.

NOTES

Chapter 16

What's Your True Passion in Life?

In this chapter, we are going to throw reality out the window for a short time! What is your passion? What do you really **love** to do? If someone were to say to you, I will pay you a very good salary/fee for your services, what would that service be? This is a very good time to start "brainstorming" with yourself and others about what you are really passionate about. Money is no object! This chapter is about your emotions. What makes you happy! ☺ **Think about this, give this some time, and sit with these ideas.** Use the creative exercises in previous chapters to help you get started. There are no right or wrong answers here. It is a place to think out loud**,;** a mental laboratory of sorts.

Why is this important you may ask? Sometimes we have a habit of only thinking in a certain way, and we need to stir things up a bit! If you are a conventional thinking person be unconventional here! If you are an unconventional thinking person, try some conventional thinking for a change. If you are an analytical thinking person, get creative and conversely, if you are a creative person think analytical. Use both sides of your brain. Think out of the box - think outside of *your* box! You will be pleasantly surprised!

Exercise:

1. What do you love to do in life?

2. Why do you like doing it?

3. What education and skills did you need to do your passion?

NOTES

NOTES

Chapter 17

How Would Like to Live Your Life?

As an extension of what was discussed in the previous chapter, what specifically would you like to do with your life? Now this may involve some research to learn about different careers, jobs, and vocations. When doing your research make sure you copy down the required skills and education to do that specific job. It's very important if you should choose to go in that direction.

You may want to be a doctor but after you research the skills and education required, it may not be the right thing for you to do**. HOWEVER,** you may like or want to be a healer of some type, explore other modalities of healing, i.e., becoming a nurse or maybe something in the holistic healing arts. There are many holistic healing modalities to choose.

The research you do here will serve you well, as it will help you get clarity on what you would like or not like to do as your "work" and/or job. The reality is, once you do discover what your work is, there will be certain skills and education required and you will need to know what they are to enable you to get the required background to do your true work.

Exercise:

1. What would you love to do **with your life** (earning a living and/or life purpose)? Forget about boundaries and just go for it!

2. What are the required skills and education you would need?

3. Identify the title, skills, and education you need and keep this as your "short list" for your potential "work"?

NOTES

NOTES

Chapter 18

Finding Your Path to Where You Want to Go

This chapter is here to assist you in getting even more clarity on the specific skills, education and experience you will need to perform your work. Once again, be open to the possibility of your work coming to you in different ways.

Once you have given some thought as to what you feel your real work is then comes the task of understanding the reality of getting to that point of implementation. Does it require more education, or more skills or more experience and/or all of the above? And then there is the cost(s) involved of making it happen. In order to do your work, these items need to be addressed.

You have made various inventories: Education (formal and informal), Skills (professional and personal skills), desired occupations, jobs, or professions. Here is where you boil it all down to specific "Work Titles". I want to be a Doctor, Chef, Reiki Master, etc. In the exercise below, write down as many Work Titles that you came up with. In later chapter, there will be discussion on how to write an effective Resume if your "work" lead you to a new job path and there will be a discussion if your work leads you to starting your own business. Either way you will need the proper tools for the marketplace; a Resume if it's a new direction in the business workplace and a Business Plan if your work is to start your own business venture.

Exercise:

1. What are your proposed "Work Titles" based on your exercises? Write them all down.

NOTES

NOTES

PART IV:

The Mental

(Our Mind)

NOTES

Chapter 19

Even More New Beginning Quotes

- "Asking is the beginning of receiving. Make sure you don't go to the ocean with a teaspoon. At least take a bucket so the kids won't laugh at you."

  - Jim Rohn

- "Take the first step in faith. You don't have to see the whole staircase, just take the first step."

  - Martin Luther King Jr.

- "With the possible exception of the equator, everything begins somewhere."

  - Peter Robert Fleming

- "The world is round and the place which may seem like the end may also be the beginning."

  - Ivy Baker Priest

- "After you've done a thing the same way for two years, look it over carefully. After five years, look at it with suspicion. And after ten years, throw it away and start all over".

  - Alfred Edward Perlman

- "As long as I am breathing, in my eyes, I am just beginning."

  - Cris Jami

- *"No ship ventures out of port if there is an expectation of the potential of sailing into harm's way. As such, you shouldn't venture down a new path until you have a series of supportive people alongside of you. These supportive people will provide on-going motivation when you hit those hurdles."*

  - Byron Pulsifer

- "All great deeds and all great thoughts have a ridiculous beginning. Great works are often born on a street corner or in a restaurant's revolving door."

  - Albert Camus

- "Although you literally took your first step when you were several months old, each time you want to make a change in your life you must take a first step that puts you in that new direction."

  - Susan Caplan McCarthy

- "Be willing to be a beginner every single morning."

  - Meister Eckhart

- "Let every dawn be to you as the beginning of life, and every setting sun be to you as its close."

  - John Ruskin

- *"If you wish to be happy right from the beginning of your day, then it is about time to leave behind your past"*

  - Lorin Hopper

Chapter 20

The Power of Our Minds

Our minds are one of the most powerful tools we have as human beings. Yet we are not taught how to use it to its full potential. Furthermore, the irony is we are using our minds more and more and our physical bodies less and less and again, there is very little teachings about how to utilize our minds properly, as well as how to rest our minds in a world full of all types of stressors and anxiety producing events.

There will be some repetition of previous information in this chapter as well as new information for a few reasons. One reason is the information is designed to build upon what you have learned, and it will now be located in one place. Another reason is that this information is extremely important to your mental wellbeing and so it is worth repeating a second time. Lastly, most "dis-ease" starts in the mind due to stress and anxiety due to modern day living (making a living, job, family, relationships, etc.) and these are practical tools that you can use immediately to help deal with stress of modern day life in both your professional and personal life.

Meditation

While there are many meditation techniques (which you are encouraged to research and learn about), they basically boil down to two methods either:

Self-Directed or Guided Meditation. Using the Self-Directed Method as stated, you are doing the meditation yourself as the example presented to you in this book and shown below. Where you are directing yourself to a meditation technique, no outside equipment, person, or anything else is required. You can perform the meditation, any time, any place (not while driving) and go into a deep state of meditation all on your own. While the Guide Meditation Method, you are being guided by a person, a recording, or any means where you are listening to a person giving you instruction. The down part about Guided Meditation Method is that you need to have access to a person, recording or things outside of yourself to do the meditation. Though I prefer the Self-Directed Method myself because I can do it anytime, anyplace, and anywhere, especially if I just left an extremely stressful situation both methods are good and helpful for healthy mental wellbeing.

Below is an example of a Self-Directed Method of Meditation used previously in this handbook:

Exercise: Meditation "1 – 2 – 3 – 4" Method of Meditation.

Meditation is aligning **Mind, Body, Emotions and Spirit**, so that these components function as one. Meditating is the practice of quieting the mind of all its chatter to enable you to be open to the thoughts of the Universe.

The benefit of this exercise is to become centered in one's self.

1. This is the **"1 – 2 – 3 – 4" Method of Meditation**.

2. Take a slow deep <u>**breath in**</u> for a count up to four – one, two, three, four.

3. Then slowly <u>**exhale out**</u> for a count up to four – one, two, three, four.

4. Take a total of 3 or 4 slow deep breaths.

5. Then just say to yourself, in your mind, **"1 – 2 – 3 – 4"** over and over again.

6. The purpose of this is to focus your mind on the counting and away from the chatter that is with us in our mind.

7. There is no right way or wrong way to perform this meditation. Do what you feel is comfortable and natural for you. There is no need for stress or strain. In time you will have no need for counting **"1 – 2 – 3 – 4"** you will be able to close your eyes and go into a calm, relaxing and peaceful meditative state.

You can do this exercise in the morning before you start your day for 5 minutes and when you end your day for 5 minutes. Then go to 10 minutes, 15 minutes, etc.

The other method mentioned is the Guided Meditation Method. You may also hear the terms, Guided Imagery, and/or Creative Visualization. These techniques are very similar in that you are you are following instructions in various forms; in writing, from a person, recording etc.

Below is an example of a Guided Method of Meditation. This is an example of a Guide Meditation for Your Life Purpose:

Creative Visualization for Your Life Purpose

1. Find a place that is quiet, and you will not be disturbed. Now close your eyes and take a nice deep breath. Take a nice deep, deep breath. Relax your mind; relax your body. You are totally calm and totally relaxed; totally calm and totally relaxed.

2. Count from four down to the number one. With every number you count, I would like you to take a deep breath, and each time say the word "relax," Relax and exhale the breath from your body. With every number you count, take a deep breath, and each time say the word "relax", relax and allow the breath to exhale from your body.

Four, take a nice deep breath (pause) and relax.

Three, take a nice deep breath (pause) and relax.

Two, take a nice deep, deep breath (pause) and relax.

One, deep breath (pause)… and relax. Relax your thoughts; relax your body.

Very good, now continue to breathe normally.

3. Now count from four down to one again. Mentally release each group of muscles that is called to your attention.

Four, release the muscles in head and face. Just release and relax. Feel your head slowly drop forward if that is comfortable for you.

Three, release the muscles in your neck and shoulders. Just release and relax any stress and any strain.

Two, release the muscles in your back and allow your hands to fall to your sides if you wish.

One, release the muscles in your stomach and feel the relaxation flow down through your legs and feet.

Like a series of dominoes, all the muscles in your body begin at the top of your head and flow into one another as each one releases and relaxes.

With every beat of your heart, with every breath that you take, you will become more relaxed, calmer, more relaxed, calmer...

... Good. Continue to use your imagination. Imagine the warm, golden sun going down into your skin and melting deeply within every cell of your body.

4. The gentle warmth flows over through your muscles, allowing them to relax. Release and relax all of the tension; all of the strain.

Feel the muscles in your neck and shoulders expand.

Notice how you feel - without stress - free in your body and mind. Your heart rate and breathing are calm and relaxed. Your muscles are totally relaxed. Totally calm, totally relaxed. Totally calm, totally relaxed.

5. Now, think about a time in the **future**. In a vision, see yourself living your life's purpose. **Write your life purpose here or what you may think your life purpose could be or might be.**

6. See yourself living your life's purpose. You are happy, fulfilled, prosperous, you are full of joy and wonderment. So happy doing your work!

7. When I count to four... you will be wide awake...feeling good and alert. Remembering everything you experienced in your visualization and able to write it down if you wish....One...you're beginning to come back...Two... feel the energy start flowing through your body...Three... moving your fingers and toes... more and more awake...feel the energy running through your body ...Four... breathing in wakeful energy... clearing your head... balancing your energies... feeling wonderful in every way..., opening your eyes... fully coming back... fully back... wide awake... and ready to go...

You can create and/or find a Guided Meditation on just about anything your need, want or desire. It is just another method of meditation.

Self-Hypnosis

Hypnosis is defined as the induction of a state of consciousness in which a person is highly receptive to suggestion or direction. Being a Hypnotherapist myself, I would further add to that definition by stating that all hypnosis is self-hypnosis and if a person does not want to change their behavior all the hypnosis sessions in the world will not make one bit of difference. Self-hypnosis takes Guided Mediation, Guided Imagery and Creative Visualization a few steps further in that you are adding a Suggestion for personal change (i.e. Stop Smoking, Lose Weight, Fear of Public Speaking, etc.) and you are adding a Post-Hypnotic Suggestion (a word, phrase or other type of tool) to remind you of the change after you have requested during the hypnosis session. Say you wanted to improve your golf swing. During a hypnosis session you would visualize yourself performing a perfect gold swing every time you played golf. **Hypnotic Suggestions** would be given to you that you are now a better golfer, seeing yourself hitting "holes in one" and the like. An example of a **Post-Hypnotic Suggestion** would be - every time you see, hear, or say the word "GOLF" you are reminded on how good of a golf player you are and how good your gold swing is. What hypnosis does is help release behavior that is no longer desired from your subconscious mind and help train your conscious mind to the desired behavior.

The steps in Self-Hypnosis are as follows:

1. Fixation: You fixate on an object to focus your mind. For example: a burning candle, a pocket watch, or anything that you can focus your gaze upon.

2. Progressive Relaxation: You mentally relax the parts of your body from your head to your toes. For example: you are relaxing and letting go of all the tension at the top of your head, the muscles around your eyes, nose, mouth, etc.

3. Guided Imagery: Visualizing in your mind the desired behavior. For example: See yourself a Professional Golfer walking on a golf course.

4. Suggestions for Desired Behavior: For example: You are a very good golfer. Every swing of your golf club produces the desired result you want. And similar types suggestions for improvement.

5. Post-Hypnotic Suggestion: A word, phrase or object that reminds the person of the desired behavior. For example: Every time you see, hear or say the word GOLF you will have a perfect golf swing.

Self-hypnosis is just another "tool for your mind" to help reach your professional and personal goals. Either teach yourself and/or work with a trained professional to help you achieve the desired behavior you want. You learn more about hypnosis you can go to the **National Guild of Hypnotists** (www.NGH.net). This is the organization that certified me, and I have been a member for over 25 years.

NOTES

Chapter 21

What are Your Personal Gifts, Talents and Attributes?

As previously stated in this segment of The Mind, some of the information discussed in this chapter and the next may seem a bit repetitive, but worth reviewing and expanding upon as it really is that important to your professional and personal future. Why are these exercises that important that they are worth repeating? The truth of the matter is that no one (if it does happen it will be extremely rare) will be asking you – And what else can you do? And what else can you do? And what else can you do? I wrote it three times to demonstrate that people in the marketplace will not be that persistent to find out from you all of your talents, skills, and personal gifts. That's your job! You have to tell the world in your professional life and your personal life what you have to offer and all of your abilities. You must be able to bang your own drum – for yourself and you are worth it!

What would you say are your natural gifts, things that just come easily to you? Are you a talented speaker, good with people; are you a good cook, good with your hands? We all have gifts, what are yours? What do people compliment you about? You can recycle some of the things mentioned in previous chapters, however, given this some deep thought. Use the meditation exercise to really ponder and reflect on your naturally born gifts.

Exercises:

1. What comes naturally to you? What is easy for you to do? Is it cooking, good with your hands, good with people?

2. Personal Gifts – We all have been given certain gifts or abilities. Do you have the gift of "gab" (being a good communicator)? Though similar to exercise 1, these are things that you just shine in doing. Are you good with your hands?

3. Talents – Have you acquired and/or perfected certain talents or skills over the years. Are you naturally a talker and a good communicator (public speaker)? Have you developed the talent for professional public speaking, or have you developed the talent for writing? Are you good with technology and technical details? Here, we are going from the general and honing into the specific.

Chapter 22

Uncover All of Your Education and Skills

We spent the previous chapters having you gather your education, skills, and life experience. In this chapter, we are going to determine what areas are useful to get you on your path. In the business world, we call these **Education and Skills Inventories**. It is our responsibilities to tell people what we do, how we can help them and what is our background in helping them. **We are going to be using the following exercises to help build your Resume (discussed in future chapter). This will also be helpful if you are planning to run your own business to see what areas of the business that you may have to hire people with certain expertise that you do not possess.** You can use the education and skills inventories from previous chapters and/or boil them down here as ones that will be useful in helping you gain greater clarity. It's your choice how you would like to do it.

Exercise:

1. **Education Inventory** – formal education, degrees, certificates, classes, self-taught.

   Make a table or spreadsheet with the following information:

   Date of Education – Subject Matter – Credential Received (Degree, Certificate, Non-Credit classes, etc.) – Institution Attended (where did you take the class) – Comments (Anything else noteworthy – Top of Class, Magna Cum Laude, etc.)

2. **Skills Inventory** – all skills, professional, self-taught skills, etc.

   Make a table or spreadsheet with the following information:

   Date Skill Learned – Skill Name – Any Credential Received? (Degree, Certificate, Non-Credit classes, SELF TAUGHT, etc.) – Institution Attended (where did you learn this skill?) – Comments (Anything else noteworthy, taught myself to write, produce and market self-published books, etc.)

NOTES

NOTES

PART V:

The Physical

(Our Body)

NOTES

Chapter 23

Yes, Even More New Beginning Quotes

1. *"Each day is a new beginning, the chance to do with it what should be done and not to be seen as simply another day to put in time."*

    - Catherine Pulsifer

2. *"Finish each day and be done with it. You have done what you could; some blunders and absurdities have crept in; forget them as soon as you can. Tomorrow is a new day; you shall begin it serenely and with too high a spirit to be encumbered with your old nonsense."*

    - Ralph Waldo Emerson

3. *"Do what you can, with what you have, where you are."*

    - Theodore Roosevelt

4. *"To make lasting change in your life . . . means that some sort of work is involved. This work means effort, continuing commitment, and the grit to keep moving forward when it becomes a lot easier to quit."*

    - Byron Pulsifer

5. *"It's never too late to go for a dream or make a change in your life. You can reinvent yourself, build a new career and maintain a positive outlook on life, at any age - even when your world is collapsing around you."*

    - Michele Laine

6. *"Nothing in the universe can stop you from letting go and starting over."*

    - Guy Finley

7. *"Don't let the lessons, the experiences of the past, dampen your enthusiasm for beginnings. Just because it's been hard doesn't mean it will always be that difficult."*

    - Melody Beattie

8. *"Just wishing does nothing for your life, but when you actually commit to taking action to make that wish come true your life takes on new meaning."*

    - Catherine Pulsifer

9. *"Unfortunately, negativity becomes habitual for many of us. However, it's never too late to turn our lives around, to laugh instead of complain."*

    - Karen Casey

10. *"The fear of failure is a common motivation killer. People don't try something new because they fear they will fail at it."*

    - Cary Bergeron

11. *"True mastery of a skill was only the beginning step to understanding it."*

    - Yoda

12. *"When you reach the end of what you should know, you will be at the beginning of what you should sense."*

    - Kahlil Gibran

Chapter 24

Eating Right, Exercise and Mother Nature

When major life events happen (births, moving, marriages, etc.) it is also a good time to evaluate other parts of your life as well. Yes, it becomes another part of your life to work, however, the benefits are that this part of your life tends to affect the other parts of your life in a very positive way. Sometimes the simplest and basic of changes in one's life can have the most profound effect. While eating right, exercise and nature are all good things in our life, they also give you the fuel to deal with other changes that you are going through.

What is meant by eating right? This discussion is by no means a substitute for meeting with your doctor and working with a trained dietary professional. Eating right mean eating food that are good for you. More natural and fresh fruits and vegetables and less processed and package foods. Watch salt and sugar intake in all of its forms. Being mindful of fried food and foods high in saturated fats. While eating in an "organic" manner is desired, it is not always a practical, cost effective and achievable goal. There are other tips and techniques to be used to help you to eat right. Going to order something, is that the best thing for you to eat? Eat a salad first, then eat half of what you ordered and eat the other half another time with another salad as well.

We all know what "good" food is versus "bad" food. This is a good time to be more mindful about what we are consuming. For me personally, since I don't cook, I'm eating more fresh fruits and vegetables and grills meats, watching the sauces I use and using a lot more spices for flavor. I feel full, satisfied and more clear headed.

Exercise. It bears repeating that this discussion is by no means a substitute for meeting with your doctor and working with a trained exercise professional. Even the mild form of exercise will do you good. The mildest form of exercise, if you can tolerate it, is walking. Walking exercises just about every part of your body. There are many benefits to walking: burning calories, strengthens your heart, boosts your energy. Exercise also has the ability to "get you out of your head" for a bit so you are not just dwelling on your problems. The benefits of walking are numerous. Just put the words "benefits of exercising" in any internet search engine and you will be amazed at the list that comes back. For me, when I go on a walk, it tends to clear my head. Problems that I'm working on that seem insurmountable, I am able to find different ways to solve them. I come back to my house with a new a better perspective on things, clear mind, and more energy.

Nature. Mother Nature. Also known as Gaia (from the Greek word meaning Earth). When your life is turned outside down and inside out, or your world does not make sense anymore, it's time to spend some time in nature. It does not mean you need to go deep into the mountains or deep into the woods or in some cave somewhere. All it means is to find yourself a little piece of nature where you live, a park, a stream, or a small piece of your backyard. If you don't have anything like this where you are, try your best to find it. Once you find a place in nature take your shoes off for a bit and feel the Mother Earth underneath you. Use the exercises that are in this handbook (meditation, creative visualization, etc.) and just let go all of your worries, stressors and concerns and let them leave your body and send them into the earth. Mother Earth will gladly take them and recycle their energy into something good! The point of spending time in nature is to help replenish your spirit, your life force. We replenish our bodies with food, our minds with positive thoughts, our heart (emotional heart) with love and one of the ways we replenish our spirits is connecting with nature. Being with and in nature will help you "ground" your thoughts and help give your different perspectives on events that you are going through.

NOTES

Chapter 25

The Real World: How Do I Move Forward with My Life?

You have been learning a lot in this hand book and sooner rather than later it will be time to go back to and be part of the "REAL WORLD" of earning a living or whatever new lifestyle you have to chosen to pursue. Moving forward after a major set back can be difficult at best and down right hard as heck at worst. So how does a person move forward after a major setback or multiple major setbacks?

First, come to terms with all that you have lost. Grieve it like a death if you have to, but don't continue to mourn and carry what was once in your life as this will not help you make room in your life to have new, even better things come into your world. Emotions are emotions, they are not logical or linear and you will feel what you feel. Do your best to acknowledge them and then let them go. Though it may be easier said then done. Letting go of your past will open doors to a new, bright and better future.

Second, understand that moving forward again is a process and with any process there are steps to follow to achieve a certain desired outcome. Understand that this may be a gradual process. Where once you were running, now you may need to crawl, before you can walk, then even speed walk before you can run. Be patient with the process. Understand the process that is required to get you where you need to go in your new life. Make the process work for you as much as possible. If one segment of the process suggested time of completion is one week and it takes you two weeks, don't let it concern you. You keep on going, inch by inch, yard by yard, mile by mile until you complete the process required to get you where you need to go. Remember the saying, "It's hard by the mile but a cinch by the inch". Rest if you must but don't you quit!

Third, set realistic goals. Set small goals that you can reach so you have a sense of accomplishment, gives you a sense of "stick to attentiveness" and know that you can do it. Don't beat yourself up if a goal is not reached in the time line you want. Reassess the goal to make sure that you set a realistic time for completion and do it again. This is a "marathon run" and not a sprint. As the old adage goes: "How do you eat an elephant? A bite at a time". If you're a vegan, you can substitute the world's largest squash in the world. ☺

Fourth, work hard and play hard. You're working hard to move forward in your new professional life work just as hard in your personal life. The "work" in this context is meant to convey the concept of "effort". Just because you're working hard towards your professional life goals doesn't mean you become reckless in your personal life. If you weren't inclined to parachute jump, go swimming with sharks and any other high risk activities doesn't mean you should start them now. All that is being said is put the effort in your personal life that you are putting into your professional life. Plan your personal life the way you plan your professional life. In your calendar, book appointments with family and friends the way you would book an appointment in your professional life. Life has a way of getting away from us with the years passing by and the people we care about the most not being involved to the degree we need, want and desire them to be.

Fifth, Celebrate! Enjoy each accomplishment, no matter how big or how small, with family and friends, extra scoop of ice cream, whatever personal reward works for you in a safe and sane manner! Enjoy the satisfaction of setting goals and achieving them. Of moving forward in your life and going to a place that was even better than the place that you just came from. You owe it to yourself because you have earned, you are worth it, and you deserve it for all your hard work, perseverance, and determination.

Moving forward after major setback(s) in a person's life may not be fun, glamorous, or exciting, but it can be done. It's a new beginning in your life, it may even be multiple new beginnings in different parts of your life both professional and personal, but it can be done. You can do it. Here's an exercise you can do: **Work hard then rest. Count your blessings (we all have them) and repeat.**

NOTES

Chapter 26

Your REAL Job – Learn How to Find It!

In this chapter we are going to discuss three very important subjects; business networking, the proper manner to write a Resume and Cover Letters. With market conditions being highly competitive for the foreseeable future, I find most people take these three topics very lightly; conversely successful people take these topics extremely seriously. Here you will learn the proper and highly effective methods to do all three and use them immediately to help you with your life purpose job, because, the truth is we live in a competitive world with those knowing what to do and doing it right, getting where they want to go and achieving all that they want to achieve. You can do it as well with the right information, tools and motivation!

What is Business Networking and Why it so Important?

Business Networking simply put is meeting people and meeting the right people to help you on your professional and personal journey. Whether you are business networking for a new job, new clients or for your social life, business and personal networking is the art and science of meeting new people and establishing relationships, be they professional or personal. The "art" is being creative in the manner in which you meet people. The "science" is once you meet someone you have a **business**

networking process (the business networking introduction) to effectively introduce yourself. Tell the listener what you do, the needs you have, how the listener can help you, how you can benefit the listener and how you can help them. All this delivered in a clear, concise manner in under 2 minutes, which happens to be the average attention span of an adult!

Business Networking (online and in-person) has become so important in the "new economy" due to more and more jobs (employment and consulting for the self-employed). Consulting is used here to indicate short and long term assignments be they employment and/or non-employment related; they are being filled through non-conventional means. Companies would rather not place advertisements in newspapers (and/or online) or pay executive recruiters and websites if they can find employees through "word of mouth" advertising (also known as business networking). Businesses would rather not deal with a long and lengthy selection process to find vendors (qualified executive recruiters). They would rather business network with other businesses to find vendors they are happy with.

In person, business networking also cuts through the "red tape" of telemarketing, mailing sales literature (or Resumes). Then waiting to see if the information has been received, and reviewed, then calling the person to see if they are available to discuss the mailed piece and so on. People do business with ***people they know, like and trust***. By business networking in person, you are starting that process and establishing relationships which will lead to you acquiring your next job, client, or personal relationship.

The Job Search Networking Introduction

The Job Search Networking Introduction also known as **"The Elevator Pitch" (or The Pitch)** – The amount of time to talk about yourself if you were riding in an elevator with someone. "The Elevator Pitch" is an important part of any business networking introduction and its purpose is to provide an overview of your professional background, your current situation, what you are looking for from the listener, how you can benefit the listener and to start a dialogue. It should be about 60 – 90 seconds in length and should answer the question of who are you, what you do, how you can help (benefit) others and what are you looking for in a clear, concise marketing pitch. It has similar characteristics to the Business Value Proposition (which will be discussed later in the handbook).

PAST – PRESENT – FUTURE - QUESTION

"The Elevator Pitch" is broken down into the **PAST** (Professional Summary), **PRESENT** (what are you doing now), **FUTURE** (your target – who/what are you looking for) and ends with a **QUESTION** (starts a dialogue). If you know what the person is looking for, then you would add the benefits of what you do. The benefit(s) can and should be added as soon as possible in your conversation.

This will answer the question **"Tell me about yourself?"** while marketing yourself in a professional non-intrusive manner to prospective employers, business networking events and others you may meet who may be able to help you with your job search.

When someone helps you always ask what you can do for them. You could be in a position to help them in a professional or personal manner.

This job search networking technique will help when you meet people in a professional setting, on the phone, at networking meetings or the beginning of interviews and even in your personal life.

Know you have a good job search networking introduction when the listeners says to you, "Tell Me More".

The following exercise is to be written out, critiqued, and practiced until it becomes a part of your introduction and networking process.

The Elevator Pitch Exercise

1. **PAST**: Write a brief career summary to include:
    a. Your most recent career history
    b. The type of work you have been performing
    c. The type of organization, industry or functional area where you performed it

2. **PRESENT:** Write a sentence in a brief, matter-of-fact way, that explains why you are presently looking for work.

3. **FUTURE:** Write a description of your target industry, position, function or role, while mentioning the organizations you are targeting.

4. **QUESTION:** Asking a question is a way to promote a dialogue between you and the listener. Write a brief question as how this person may be of help to you.

5. **The Job Search Networking Introduction:** Put it all together in a clear, simple to understand and flowing manner.

Business Networking Contact Form

Date: _____ Event: _____

Contact Name: _____ Contact Title: _____

Phone: _____ Email: _____

Mobile Phone: _____ FAX: _____

Company Name: _____ Website: _____

Company Address: _____

City: _____ State: _____ Zip: _____

Type of Assistance (How Can This Person Help Me?) Circle All That Apply:

- Industry Information   - Introduction to Companies - Job/Project Lead

- Company Information   - Provide Contact Name(s)   - Other

_____

How Can I Help Them? _____

Notes/Comments:

_____

_____

_____

_____

Follow Up:

_____

The Resume

What is the real purpose of a Resume? You may think the purpose of a Resume is to get you a job. **In truth, a well prepared Resume gets you an interview and an interview gets you a job.** People hire people, not Resumes!

What should be on your Resume? The content of your Resume is important to help you get that phone call for that all important interview.

The Different Styles of Resumes:

Chronological

Functional

Combination

The style most accepted and used in today's marketplace is the **Chronological format.** The Functional and Combination Resume, though used, are frowned upon by hiring authorities and executive recruiters. The main reason is that these types of Resumes are difficult to read and understand.

They do have their place in the job search but should be used with caution. Though Sample Resumes of the different formats are provided in this chapter, you may want to learn more about Functional Resumes and suggest you perform research on the Internet.

Action Verbs

Employers hire people who can perform skilled tasks for them. Your Resume should be written to clearly and concisely communicate the valuable skills that they need. Your future employer is extremely interested in your accomplishments. If you have **accomplished work objectives with results** in the past, chances are you will be a strong contributor to your new employer in the future.

You want to demonstrate that you played an **active role** in your career and were not a spectator who watched from the sidelines.

Look at the following statement and choose the stronger word. "*Assisted* the Human Resources Department in writing the employee handbook", **OR** "*Collaborated* with the Human Resources Department in writing the employee handbook". *Assisted* sounds like you supplied paper for the copy machine, got coffee and picked up lunch, while *Collaborated* infers you were working shoulder to shoulder with Human Resources Department to construct the employee handbook, doing valuable research and other important tasks.

The following list of verbs is by no means complete. It is a good place to start your search for strong action verbs/words to describe what you have accomplished.

Adapted	Designed	Investigated	Protected
Advised	Developed	Judged	Questioned
Administered	Diagnosed	Learned	Read
Analyzed	Directed	Lectured	Reasoned
Applied	Discovered	Led	Recommended
Approved	Displayed	Listened	Reconciled
Arranged	Drew	Located	Recorded
Assembled	Edited	Maintained	Recruited
Assessed	Encouraged	Managed	Reduced
Assisted	Estimated	Measured	Reinforced
Balanced	Established	Mediated	Reorganized
Budgeted	Evaluated	Memorized	Repaired
Classified	Expedited	Mentored	Reported
Clarified	Followed	Monitored	Researched
Coached	Forged	Motivate	Restored
Collected	Formulated	Negotiated	Retrieved
Coordinated	Founded	Nurtured	Revised
Communicated	Gathered	Operated	Reviewed
Compared	Generated	Observed	Scheduled

Compiled	Guided	Organized	Shaped
Completed	Handled	Participated	Simplified
Computed	Helped	Originated	Solved
Conceived	Identified	Perceived	Spoke
Conceptualized	Implemented	Performed	Synthesized
Conducted	Improved	Persisted	Streamlined
Confronted	Improvised	Persuaded	Studied
Constructed	Increased	Planned	Supervised
Contrasted	Influenced	Prepared	Supported
Controlled	Initiated	Presented	Taught
Comprehended	Integrated	Processed	Tested
Coordinated	Inspired	Produced	Trained
Counseled	Installed	Programmed	Treated
Created	Instructed	Promoted	Tutored
Decided	Interpreted	Proposed	Validated
Defined	Interviewed	Proved	Volunteered
Demonstrated	Invented	Provided	Wrote

SAMPLE ACTION VERBS LISTED BY FUNCTIONAL SKILL AREA

COMMUNICATION	CREATIVE	DETAIL ORIENTED	INVESTIGATING / RESEARCH
Aided	Acted	Analyzed	Calculated
Arbitrated	Abstracted	Arranged	Catalogued
Advised	Adapted	Approved	Collected
Clarified	Composed	Classified	Computed
Consulted	Conceptualized	Collated	Correlated
Contributed	Created	Compared	Conducted
Cooperated	Designed	Complied	Critiqued
Coordinated	Developed	Documented	Diagnosed
Counseled	Directed	Enforced	Discovered
Debated	Drew	Follow	Examined
Defined	Fashioned	through	Experimented
Directed	Generated	Met	Extrapolated
Enlisted	Illustrated	deadlines	Evaluated
Explained	Imagined	Prepared	Identified

Expressed	Improvised	Processed	Gathered
Helped	Integrated	Recorded	Inspected
Influenced	Innovated	Retrieved	Interpreted
Informed	Painted	Set	Investigated
Inspired	Performed	Priorities	Monitored
Interpreted	Planned	Systemized	Observed
Interviewed	Problem solved	Tabulated	Organized
Mediated			Proved
Merged	Shaped		Reviewed
Negotiated	Wrote		Surveyed
Promoted	Visualized		Tested
Recommended	Synthesized		
Represented			
Resolved			
Suggested			

ORGANIZING	PROVIDING SERVICE	MANUAL SKILLS	FINANCIAL
Achieved	Advised	Arranged	Administered
Assigned	Attended	Assembled	Allocated
Administered	Cared	Bound	Analyzed
Consulted	Coached	Built	Appraised
Contracted	Coordinated	Checked	Audited
Controlled	Counseled	Classified	Budgeted
Decided	Delivered	Controlled	Calculated
Coordinated	Demonstrated	Constructed	Computed
Delegated	Explained	Cut	Developed
Developed	Furnished	Designed	Evaluated
Directed	Generated	Droved	Figured
Established	Inspected	Developed	Maintained
Led	Installed	Handled	Managed
Negotiated	Issued	Installed	Performed
Organized	Mentored	Invented	Planned
Planned	Referred	Maintained	
Prioritized	Repaired	Prepared	
Produced	Provided	Monitored	
Recommended	Purchased	Operated	
Reported	Submitted	Repaired	
		Tested	

OARS - Objective/Action/Result/Statement

It's all about accomplishments. What have you done for anyone lately?

The **OARS** formula will help you describe your professional accomplishments.

O - The business **OBJECTIVE** (problem, challenge, etc.) which you were responsible for.

A - The **ACTION** you took to solve the business objective usually begins with an *ACTION VERB* (See section).

R - What was the **RESULT** that you obtained measured in some type of quantifiable terms (saved or made a company money, saved time, increased productivity, reduced costs, etc.)?

S - The **STATEMENT** you put together from the above three items.

<u>**OARS Accomplishment Statement:**</u>

Objective + Action + Result = Statement

RESULTS MAY BE EXPRESSED IN:

Dollars – Percentages – Work Hours – Ratios – Quotas - People

Money Saved – Money Earned

Time Saved – Process Improved

Winning Back Lost Customers

Improving Morale to Increase Productivity

AND/OR

Improving Morale to Reduce Employee Turnover

Did You Meet or Exceed:
Deadlines, Budgets,
Expectations, Goals, and Objectives

Did You Increase:
Productivity, Customer Satisfaction,
Market Share, Efficiency, Effectiveness, Customer Retention,
Morale, New Business, and Quality

Did You Decrease:
Turnaround Time, Cycle Time, Down Time,
Problems, Waste, Debt, Back Log, Inventory, Man Hours,
Employee Turnover, Accounts Payable,
Product or Service Costs, Customer Complaints

The following **OARS** Statements are examples from Resumes. Good **OARS** Statements use action verbs. The order is not so important as to all items (Objective/Action/Result) are identified.

1. **Increased** sales through new prospects and installed base accounts, expanding sales by 30%.

2. **Created** and **conducted** interview training program for managers reducing candidate interview process by 25%.

3. **Implemented** order processing system which increased efficiency in the customer service department when interfacing with clients.

<u>OARS Accomplishment Statement:</u>
Objective + Action + Result = Statement

The OARS Statement does not have go exactly as mentioned above but it MUST contain all the elements (pieces) in your statement.

Components of the Resume

The components of the Resume should include:

- Heading

- Summary (Professional or Executive)

- Work History with Achievements

- Professional Development/Additional Skills

- Education

In this section there will be a discussion of each **Component of the Resume** with examples to illustrate their usage.

Heading

The **Heading** section contains your contact information: name, address, telephone numbers with area code and e-mail address. It is very important that potential employers and recruiters are able to contact you. Make sure your contact information is accurate and you have email, voicemail or other methods of receiving your messages. It is a good practice, while you are in your job search, to make sure you have a professional sounding message on your voicemail.

Heading (Example)

John Smith   212-555-1234

---

100 Main Street, Anytown, State 12345   e-Mail: jsmith@hotmail.com

Professional Summary

The **Professional Summary** section contains the main points of your professional qualifications. It is a snapshot of your experience, skills, and work traits. It is a good place to start placing your "keywords" (words that are used by resume databases and hiring authorities). Keywords are skills, education and qualifications that indicate your professional abilities. The more keywords you have on your Resume the greater the chance your resume will be selected for review. The Professional Summary should contain no more than six (6) lines.

Below are two styles of writing the **Professional Summary**. Pick a style that you prefer. Remember that the purpose of the **Professional Summary** is to give the reader an overview of your professional skills and ability.

Professional Summary

A management consultant with extensive experience in project management, information technology and implementation of financial software solutions. Performed consulting for Fortune 500 clients and have expertise in: business analysis, requirement definition, technical design specifications and software evaluations. Organized, analytical, results-oriented, and excellent interpersonal skills.

Professional Summary

A management consultant with extensive experience in project management, information technology and implementation of financial software solutions.   Organized, analytical, results-oriented, and excellent interpersonal skills.

Consulting	Programming	Mentoring
SKILL	**SKILL**	**SKILL**
SKILL	**SKILL**	**SKILL**

Both styles are acceptable. Some people prefer to work with one style over the other.

Professional Summary (Examples)

Corporate Administrative Assistant/Executive Secretary with extensive experience at the highest executive level. Major strengths in organization and detail, verbal and written communications and all aspects of managerial travel. Works independently. Exceptionally good judgment. A well-organized, dependable professional who takes pride in her work.

Senior Financial executive with wide-ranging experience at Fortune 10 Company and Big 6 accounting firm. Expertise includes strategic planning, budgeting, financial reporting, financial analysis & modeling, acquisitions/ divestitures, financial controls and project management. Innovative financial and operational problem-solver. Excellent interpersonal skills.

An Information Technology professional with extensive experience in developing IBM's Customer Relationship Management (CRM) solutions on enterprise systems. Major strengths include problem solving skills and programming logic for mainframe applications. Ability to translate customer needs into technology solutions. Team player with ability to learn and apply new skills in a short amount of time.

A Senior Management/Marketing Professional with experience building profits in a broad range of product and service businesses. Major strengths include:

Strategic Planning	Customer Focused	Marketing Management
Problem Solving	Interpersonal Skills	Organizational Skills
Analytical Skills	Computer Skills	Accounting Skills

Work History with Achievements

This section **Work History with Achievements** (or **Professional History** or **Professional Experience** or **Work History**) is presenting to the reader, your various employers, location of employment, dates of employment, responsibilities, and accomplishments. **Written in reverse chronological order**, listing your most recent job first, then next job before that, then next job before that, etc.

This section supports and gives the reader the details of your **Professional Summary**. In this area you demonstrate your responsibilities and show your accomplishments, position by position, going back no more than twenty (20) years. The hiring authority is very concerned about your most recent position as those skills are currently being used and/or are fresh in your work history, and, to a lesser extent, the positions and skills five (5) years before that and to an even lesser extent, ten (10) years before that. Not to say that your work history is not important, but the "perception" is that older positions and skills are not as current or "fresh" as your most recent position.

Work History with Achievements (Example)

Acme Inc., New York, New York　　　　　　**2000-2020**

A Fortune 500 company specializing in telecommunications and technology.

Senior Marketing Director

Responsible for all marketing activities in the northeast division and management of the marketing team.

- Implemented major accounts program under time and budget saving department 3 months and $100,000 in implementation services fees.

- Created nationwide marketing programs which aided sales team to generate $2 million dollars in revenue in 6 months.

- Analyzed marketing proposal work flow and created new policies and procedures resulting in faster turn-around times for proposals to sales team.

- **OARS Accomplishment: Objective + Action + Result = Statement**

Professional Development/Additional Skills

The section **Professional Development/Additional Skills** contains skills and training acquired in a non-academic environment (i.e., not in a University, College or High School). You may possess business skills and education that may be very valuable to your future employer, though not acquired in an academic environment, important none the less.

For example, you may have acquired computer skills on the job over a period of years. Or you have been trained in a certain selling methodology like "Miller-Heiman Strategic Selling".

Remember, only business-related skills and education, are what your future employer and recruiters are interested in. That's the additional value you bring to them.

Professional Development (Example)

Sales Training, Miller-Heiman – Strategic and Conceptual Selling

Meeting Planner, Certified Meeting Planner, American Planning Association

Seminar Leader, Certified Seminar Leader, American Seminar Leaders Association

Additional Skills (Example)

Computer Skills, Microsoft – Word, Excel, PowerPoint, and Outlook

Foreign Language, Spanish – Read, Write, Speak

Notary Public, Licensed in State of New Jersey until June 2025

Education

The **Education** section is where your formal higher education (e.g. PhD, Master's, Bachelor's, and Associates Degree) is placed. Only completed degrees are to be mentioned. High school diploma can be shown if you have not had a college education. Dates of graduation can be listed however there are pros and cons to doing so.

Education (Example)

M.S., Engineering, SUNY – University of Albany

B.S., Business, Rutgers College

A.S., Computer Science, Nassau Community College

Sample Resumes

John Smith   **212-555-1212**

100 Main Street, Anytown, State 12345   e-Mail: jsmith@hotttmail.com

SAMPLE CHRONOLOGICAL RESUME

PROFESSIONAL SUMMARY

General Manager and Senior Marketing Executive with an extensive record of achievement with Fortune 1000 companies including Information and Financial Services, Telecommunications and Consumer Products. Produces outstanding results through leadership, vision, organization development, communications, and strategic alliances and managing overall profitability.

PROFESSIONAL EXPERIENCE

Automatic Data Processing, Inc., Parsippany, New Jersey   **1997-2001**

Senior Director Marketing, eBusiness Services, Major Accounts Division

- Built and maintained key alliances instrumental in delivering innovative client solutions with minimal expense and reduced time to market.
- Developed and launched the Major Accounts portal, a comprehensive business to employee, web-based, self-service application targeted at mid-market employers and their employees. Currently in pilot in the Atlanta and Los Angeles regions.
- Launched a web-based travel and expense reporting and tracking application. Exceeded initial revenue and client acquisition targets.
- Introduced a voluntary employee, and payroll deduction insurance program in five key regions. Currently in phased national rollout.
- Created the Y2K client awareness and customer care education campaign. Achieved a "zero incidence" target.
- Developed the Valued Client Loyalty Program for the Miami and Dallas regions resulting in a $1.5M revenue gain in client retention over 18 months.

Nynex Long Distance Co., New York, New York   **1996-1997**

Assistant Vice President, Consumer Markets

- Developed the consumer market strategy and test launch of the Nynex Long Distance Company (NLD). Receive award for launching NLD on time and within budget strengthening the company's position in the Bell Atlantic merger.
- Identified ethnic and general market profiles resulting in focused communications and higher than expected direct response.
- Implemented a channel strategy lowering acquisition cost and expected consumer churn.

John Smith   212-555-1212

Western Union Financial Services, Paramus, New Jersey   1990-1996
   Director, Development, 1992-1996

- Introduced the first pre-paid Phone Card resulting on $8M first year revenue.
- Developed a long-term plan to lower cost, increasing profitability over 18 months by $5M.
- Initiated process to identify new business opportunities, establishing a critical path, benchmarks, and selection and success criteria.

   Product Manager, Consumer Money Transfer, 1991-1992

- Developed and executed business plan generating over $200M in revenue.
- Managed $20M budget for network and spot television, African American radio, local marketing, and market research.
- Developed over 250 customized key network volume building programs reversing a 13% decline in major markets to a 3% increase. Received the 1992 President's Award.

   Product Manager, Message Services, 1990-1991

- Conducted market research among users, identifying key product weaknesses.
- Spearheaded strategy to re-position Telegram and improve product quality resulting in a 40% increase in Telegram delivery and a $.3M decrease in customer refunds.

Nabisco Brands, Inc., East Hanover, New Jersey   1985-1990
Marketing Manager, Biscuit Division, Snack Cracker Category, 1988-1990

- Introduced Harvest Crisps, the first national low fat, cholesterol and sodium free snack cracker. Achieved $25M in year one sales.
- Received 1990 Marketing Excellence Award for Best New Product Introduction.

Merck, Sharp & Dohme, West Point, Pennsylvania   1984
Market Research, Summer Intern

EDUCATION

MBA, Concentration in Marketing, June 1985
The Wharton School, University of Pennsylvania, Philadelphia, Pennsylvania

BA, Economics and French, Dean's List,
May 1980 Tufts University, Medford, Massachusetts

John Smith	212-555-1212
100 Main Street, Anytown, State 12345	e-Mail: jsmith@hotttmail.com

SAMPLE CHRONOLOGICAL RESUME
with Skills from Summary Highlighted

PROFESSIONAL SUMMARY

A professional scientist with over ten year's experience in biochemical and pharmaceutical fields. Major strengths include methods development, research, analysis, and training. Precise, organized, and flexible.

Chemical analysis	R.M. testing	Implementation of Worksheet
Wet Chemistry	Formulation	Protein Purification
Method Development	Equipment Calibration	Production
Method Validation	Environmental Health	Engineering

PROFESSIONAL EXPERIENCE

Bausch and Lomb, Valley Cottage, NY　　　　　　　　　　　　　　　　　1994-2000

Research Scientist/Formulator
Performed methods development, stability studies, validated methods, and performed crossover studies. Trained staff on assay methodology and test instrument use. Selected as Environmental Health and Safety Coordinator.

- Created and introduced worksheet procedure to focus and facilitate FDA inspections of new drugs applications.
- Analyzed various color reformulations of smaller dosage Diamox Capsule, which increased differentiation versus generics and expanded international acceptance.
- Initiated a plan to get certified to calibrate and perform preventive maintenance on lab instruments, eliminating the cost of outsourcing.
- Established procedure to document training received by staff to facilitate FDA audits.
- Developed an improved method for SDS-PAGE, which eliminated "shadow" on the gels.
- Successfully trained, cross-trained, and managed a small group of analytical chemists while supervisor was out on maternity leave.

Pfizer Pharmaceuticals, Brooklyn, NY　　　　　　　　　　　　　　　　　1993-1994
Analyst
Tested raw materials, in-proc Tested raw materials, in-process and finished products using thin layer chromatography.

- Increased efficiency of TLC testing by 33%, allowing HPLC and dissolution work to be done concurrently.

John Smith   212-555-1212

American Home Products, Pearl River, NY   1992-1993

- Control Chemist
Analyzed raw materials using USP, NF and in-house test methods.

- Trained new employees and cross-trained chemists from different groups in wet chemistry, resulting in a 50% reduction of the 200-hour testing backlog within 4 months.

Purdue Frederick, Yonkers, NY   1991-1992

- Assistant Scientist
Studied the performance of narcotic dosages and particularly evaluated the content, uniformity, stability, and dissolution of morphine.

- Performed calibration of HPLC systems to ensure GMP compliance.

Bayer Diagnostics, Tarrytown, NY   1986-1990

Biochemical Technician, 1987-1990
Purified and characterized antibodies in-house. Assayed liquid and dry blend reagents for blood analyzers and performed quality/stability testing of reagents and equipment to ensure all elements met specifications.

Product Engineering Technician, 1986
Developed techniques for extruding Teflon tubing of various dimensions for the CHEM-1 instrument and trained production technicians to prepare all tubing necessary to support CHEM-1 production.

PUBLICATIONS

Co-author of Clarification of Ascites Fluid, *Biotechniques*. Volume 10, No. 4 (1991)

CERTIFICATIONS

Maintenance and Trouble Shooting of HP 1100LC and HP GC 6890, Hewlett Packard, 1999
Performing IQ, OQ & PV on instruments, Hewlett Packard, 1999

EDUCATION

BS, Chemistry - University State of New York, 1991
AAS, Chemical Technology - Westchester Community College, 1983

John Smith   **212-555-1212**

100 Main Street, Anytown, State 12345   e-Mail: jsmith@hotttmail.com

SAMPLE: CHRONOLOGICAL - ONE COMPANY ONLY – DIFFERENT POSITIONS

SUMMARY

Financial executive with extensive experience and proven track record in the pharmaceutical industry. Directed finance reengineering team for the U.S. pharmaceutical business ($3 billion in revenues), which achieved significant improvements in the budgeting process and the monthly financial closing process. Also, led an SAP global finance team, which laid the foundation (common configuration) for successful implementation of SAP as an ERP system. Recognized for accomplishments in reengineering and change management in two recent articles in STRATEGIC FINANCE.

PROFESSIONAL EXPERIENCE

Hoffman-La Roche, Inc. Nutley, NJ   1977-2000

Director-Finance Transformation, 1999-2000

- Created a new department with a $950,000 annual budget focused on transforming finance from transition processing to decision and support fostering continuous improvement in the planning process. Designed and implemented job competencies for finance, developed and delivered training
- Programs for the finance and IT, coordinated the Roche North American finance benchmarking process, generated finance wide communications, and assisted the SAP organization in ongoing training.

Director-Finance Reengineering, 1997-1999

- Led a Finance Reengineering initiative utilizing activity based costing which redirected finance activities towards more of a process orientation, customer focus, pro-activity, and business partnering were identified as key attributes.
- Achieved a 50% time saving for management in the planning process resulting in a $5 million cost improvement over two budget cycles.
- Reduced monthly closing cycle from seven days to five days (pre-SAP)

Director Finance Informatics, 1996-1999

- Saved $150,000 annually by outsourcing ongoing maintenance for legacy systems.
- Proactively transitioned selected employees onto SAP enterprise-wide team.

John Smith   212-555-1212

SAP Business Process Team Leader-Pharmaceuticals Order Billing Process, 1996-1997

- Generated procedure streamlining enhancement prioritization process.

SAP Global Finance Team Leader-SAP Kernel Upgrade, 1996-1995

- Directed global team in SAP upgrade, resulting in quality, on time, under budget product which met/exceeded all customer requirements.

Director-Customer Financial Services, 1994-1995

- Directed Accounts Payable, Credit and Collections, and Accounts Receivable departments.
- Saved $250,000 annually by outstanding T&E processing to Gelco, reducing T&E audits from %100 to %10, and initiated Imaging for A/P transactions.

Director-Capital Accounting and Financial Analysis, 1993-1994

- Developed initial Capital Expenditure and Procedure Manual which both documented and streamlined the process.
- Created combined local and global Request for Capital Expenditure procedure.

Director Financial Analysis and Corporate Budgeting, 1988-1992

- Coordinated and consolidated strategic plan and budgets and prepared presentations for senior management for Pharmaceuticals, Vitamins and Fine Chemicals, Diagnostics, and Biomedical Laboratories businesses.

Manager-Fixed Asset Accounting, 1984-1987

Manager-Financial Reporting, 1983-1984

Sr. Financial Analyst-Operations Analysis, 1980-1982

Financial Analyst-Project Financial Services,   1977-1980

CERTIFICATION

Licensed as a Certified Public Accountant in New Jersey

EDUCATION

MBA, – St. Louis University, BS, Accounting **–St. Peter's College**

John Smith   **212-555-1212**

100 Main Street, Anytown, State 12345   e-Mail: jsmith@hotttmail.com

SAMPLE FUNCTIONAL RESUME

PROFILE

General manager and senior marketing executive with an extensive record of achievement in Fortune 500, leveraged buyout and start-up organization. Produces outstanding results through leadership, strategic vision, organizational development, communication and execution. Experience includes extensive P&L background, business development, new product development turnaround management, mergers, and acquisitions.

ACCOMPLISHMENTS

- In one year, rebuilt a virtually nonexistent new product pipeline for Reckitt & Colman PLC, with winning concepts in development for market introduction over the next three years.

- Developed and launched *Resolve Fabric Refresher* in record time to gain key market position in a new category, generating $35MM in incremental revenue in Year 1.

- Developed and implemented, as part of the executive team, a new corporate infrastructure establishing Personal Care Group, Inc. as a stand-alone company. Reduced overhead by 34% or $7.4MM, versus prior corporate levels.

- Led a newly recruited organization to two years of double-digit increases in operating profit by revitalizing basic product lines and delivering unprecedented new product results in the company's five core businesses.

- Secured corporate approval of a three-year investment plan, assembled a cross-functional team and successfully developed, test marketed and launched *Ogilvie* Tender Color hair color on a regional basis.

- Developed and implemented new strategic direction for the base *Ogilvie* Home Permanent business, reversing three-year decline in brand sales and increasing profits by 19%.

- Developed and implemented strategic plan which reversed declining sales volume of Max Factor's Women's Fragrance business and delivered $3.5MM profit for businesses that had previously been unprofitable.

- Positioned and introduced Imari brand, which generated sales of $53MM, 40% above plan, and remains Avon's most successful fragrance entry to date.

John Smith   212-555-1212

EXPERIENCE

CRYSTAL JOURNEY CANDLES, LLC, Essex, CT, 2000-Present
Consultant, Marketing/Business Development

RECKITT & COLMAN PLC, Wayne, NJ, 1998-1999
Vice President, Marketing, New Products, North America

PERSONAL CARE GROUP, INC., Montvale, NJ, 1996-1998
Vice President, Marketing

EASTMAN KODAK CP./L&F PRODUCTS, INC., Montvale, NJ, 1989-1995
Group Product Manager, Personal Products Division

REVLON INC./MAX FACTOR & CO., Stamford, CT, 1985-1989
Director of Marketing, Women's Fragrance

AVON PRODUCTS, INC., New York, NY, 1978-1985
Senior Product Manager, Women's Fragrance, 1983-1985
Senior Quality Engineer, Corporate Quality Assurance, 1978-1981

YARDLEY OF LONDON, INC., Atlanta, GA, 1976-1978
Project Leader, Research and Development

NATIONAL SERVICE INDUSTRIES, INC, Atlanta, GA, 1974-1976

Quality Control Chemist, Research and Development

EDUCATION

B.S. Biology/Chemistry, cum laude, 1974
North Georgia College & State University, Dahlonega, GA

Cover Letters

It is a Cover Letter that you send to a potential employer along with your Resume. A Cover Letter is important because, among other things, (1) it will tell the recipient for whom the Resume is intended, (2) it can elaborate on your knowledge of the company and your desire to work for it, and (3) it allows you to "name drop" if you know someone within that company.

Each Cover Letter must be produced for a specific employer. You can recycle some of the text for Cover Letters within the same industry, but each letter should contain a reference to something unique about the employer/company and what he/she/it has done.

Never **send a Resume without a Cover Letter as the recipient will not know and/or forget what position you were applying for or to whom the Resume and Cover Letter should be forwarded to.**

Cover Letter Template

The **Cover Letter Template** will show you a standard method to use in creating a Cover Letter for any opportunity. It is broken up into three sections with each section having a specific purpose. In the following page a Cover Letter Template with each section being described. Your Cover Letters should not exceed one page as anything long usually will not be read by prospective employers.

After **The Cover Letter Template** you will see samples of several other types of Cover Letter and one in particular that has produced more results for the candidates that have submitted this format shown.

Cover Letter Template

Name
Address, Apt. #
City, State Zip
Phone:
FAX:
Email:

Date

Name, Title
Company Name
Address
City, State Zip

Dear Mr. or Ms. XXXXX:

Paragraph 1

- **Mention who you are and why you are contacting their organization.**

Each paragraph should not contain more than 5 to 6 lines. Be short, hard hitting and to the point to capture the reader's attention as soon as possible!

Paragraph 2

- **Mention what you have accomplished for other companies and/or what you can do for their company, based on research you performed about their company.**

Here you should have bulleted statements about your accomplishments (O/A/R/S = Objective/Action/Result = Statement) or what problem you can help the company solving with your background. You want to demonstrate how you can save a company time, money and increase their productivity.

Paragraph 3

- **Call to Action! Here is where you some action to happen!**

In the last paragraph you are thanking the person for their time, requesting an interview, or telling the person you will be calling next week to follow up on this letter.

Sincerely yours,

John Smith

Enc.: Resume

REMEMBER: The purpose of the Cover Letter and Resume is not to get you a job but to get you an interview. An interview gets you a job! Keep you letters short and to the point and always demonstrate value – what you can do for them!

Sample Cover Letters

John Smith   **212-555-1212**

100 Main Street, Anytown, State 12345   e-Mail: jsmith@hotttmail.com

SAMPLE COVER LETTER

January 1, 2020

Mr. Michael C. Marvis, President
Marvis Construction Company
1121 Jackson Blvd.
Akron, Ohio 24520

Dear Mr. Marvis:

    Your recently completed shopping complex on Eighth Avenue is well designed and compatible with the existing neighborhood. I am particularly impressed with how you placed the parking area next to the main access points for the restaurant and theatre complex.

    I am especially interested in your work because my background is in architectural drafting. I know good design, and I want to associate with a firm that will fully use my talents. My qualifications include:

- Three years of architectural drafting experience; helped develop plans for $14 million of residential and commercial construction.
- Three years handling all aspects of construction, building and installing cabinets, reconstructing commercial building, pouring concrete.
- Collected and evaluated data for controlling quality of construction.
- Trained as a draftsman.

    At present I am seeking an opportunity to use my skills in developing projects similar to your Eighth Avenue shopping complex.

    I would appreciate an opportunity to meet with you to discuss our mutual interests. I will call your office next week to arrange a convenient time.

I look forward to meeting you.

Sincerely yours,

John Smith

John Smith	**212-555-1212**
100 Main Street, Anytown, State 12345	e-Mail: jsmith@hotttmail.com

SAMPLE COVER LETTER

January 1, 2020

Mr. Michael C. Marvis, President
Marvis Construction Company
1121 Jackson Blvd.
Akron, Ohio 24520

Dear Mr. Marvis:

 In today's competitive climate in the banking industry, one of the most important resources a bank can have is a staff member well qualified in the area of Customer Relations – not only to attract new customers, but also to retain those already on board. My background and experience make me uniquely fitted for such a position.

 In the past fifteen years, at Chase Manhattan Bank, I have effectively supervised and managed twelve branches. My accomplishments include the following:

- $250,000 in money market fund sales over 9-month period.
- Weekly sales of 10-15 certificates of deposit.
- Resolution of 99% of all customer complaints to the satisfaction of both bank and customer.
- Solution of numerous operational problems to everyone's satisfaction.
- Minimal loss of money in seven hold-ups involving four branches; major factor was compliance by staff to my security instructions.

 I would welcome the opportunity to discuss with you how my experience and abilities might make a substantial contribution to your operation. With that in mind I will call your office next week to arrange a mutually convenient time for us to meet.

Very truly yours,

John Smith

John Smith   **212-555-1212**

100 Main Street, Anytown, State 12345   e-Mail: jsmith@hotttmail.com

SAMPLE COVER LETTER

January 1, 2020

Mr. Michael C. Marvis, President
Marvis Construction Company
1121 Jackson Blvd.
Akron, Ohio 24520

Dear Mr. Marvis:

    Advanced Technology's word processing equipment is the finest on the market today. I know, because I have used different systems over the past eight years. Your company is the type of organization I would like to be associated with.

    Over the next few months I will be seeking a sales position with an information processing company. My technical, sales, and administrative experience include:

- **Technical:** Eight years operating Mag card and high-speed printers: IBM 6240, Mag A, I, II, IBM 6640, and Savin word processor.
- **Sales:** Recruited clients, maintained inventory; received and filled orders; improved business-community relations.
- **Administrative:** Planned and re-organized word processing center; created new tracking and filing system; initiated time and cost studies which reduced labor costs by $30,000 and improved efficiency of operations.

    In addition, I have a bachelor's degree in communication with emphasis on public speaking, interpersonal communication, and psychology.

    Your company interests me very much. I would appreciate an opportunity to meet with you to discuss how my qualifications can best meet your needs. Therefore, I will call your office next Monday, January 18, to arrange a meeting with you at a convenient time.

    Thank you for your time and consideration.

Sincerely,

John Smith

John Smith	212-555-1212
100 Main Street, Anytown, State 12345	e-Mail: jsmith@hotttmail.com

SAMPLE COVER LETTER
Response to Advertised Position (Best Response Rate)

January 1, 2020

Mr. Michael C. Marvis, President
Marvis Construction Company
1121 Jackson Blvd
Akron, Ohio 24520

Dear Mr. Marvis:

 Your advertisement on Monster.com, on June 9, 2020, for an Assessment Coordinator seems to perfectly match my background and experience. As the International Brand Coordinator for Kahlua, I coordinated meetings, prepared presentations, and materials, organized a major off-site conference, and supervised an assistant. I believe that I am an excellent candidate for this position as I have illustrated below.

YOUR REQUIREMENTS	MY QUALIFICATIONS
A highly motivated, diplomatic, flexible, quality-driven professional	Successfully managed project teams involving different business units. The defined end results were achieved on every project.
Exceptional organizational skills and attention to detail	Planned the development and launch of the Kahula Heritage Edition bottle series. My former manager would leave the "details" and follow-through to me. Attended Coverdale Project Management training.
College degree and minimum 3 years relevant business experience	B.A. from Vassar College (1994). 5+ years business experience in productive, professional environments
Computer literacy	Extensive knowledge of Windows & Macintosh Applications

 I am interested in this position because it fits well with my new career focus in the human resources field. Currently, I am enrolled in NYU's adult career planning and development certificate program and working at Lee Hecht Harrison.

 I have enclosed my resume to provide more information on my strengths and career achievements. If after reviewing my material you believe that there is a match, please call me. Thank you for your consideration.

Sincere regards,
John Smith

The Hidden Job Market

Over 80% of today's jobs are not advertised or posted on websites. The main reason has got to do with keeping hiring costs low. There are costs involved in posting jobs on the internet, placing an ad in the paper, or hiring an executive recruiter. Furthermore, hiring takes up quite a bit of a company's time; to review candidate resumes, schedule interviews, and then having hiring meetings to determine which candidate to make an offer for the position. Then, if that particular candidate does not accept, the position, the process continues, and may even have to begin all over again.

With all that said, **the best job to apply for, is a job that no one is applying for.** What this means is you want to present yourself to company and act as your own "executive recruiter". You want to do the appropriate research about a company, the people in that company and their needs and present yourself to them. Sometimes you may be the right candidate for a job, applying at the right time just when they have a particular need and your timing was just right! There are even instances where jobs have been created for the right candidate. Why did that happen? The candidate offered so much value and understood the company's issues so well, the company or organization would be foolish to let such a talented and productive individual get away from them and possibly fall into the hands of their competition!

There are many methods to tap into the hidden job market. As I previously discussed, business networking is one method. When we talk about business networking we mean, "face to face" and online business networking. Both have their unique advantages. The main things to remember when business networking is to not to get frustrated and give up, and make sure you are business networking with the right people in your field. If you are looking to land a job or a client in the technology industry, don't be business networking with people that sell truck parts because it is highly unlikely that they have contacts in the technology industry. The main thing to remember about business networking using either method, is to be business networking with likeminded people in your field so that you can find and hear about opportunities and also you can be found and people hear about you. **If someone is looking for someone just like you and they don't know about you then they will never find you and then obliviously not hire you.**

Usual Methods and the Internet

What should not be discounted are the usual methods of job search, business networking with family and friends, checking the local/regional newspapers and the internet. **When seeking employment there is no one particular method that works all of the time, the best method is the method that works for you!** When using the internet, it is a good strategy to post your resume on the major job boards like, i.e., Monster.com, HotJobs.com, etc. Also **look for job boards (websites) that deal with your specific industry**. If you are an accountant for example, a good place to post your resume would be on AccountingJobs.com as the jobs on this website are specifically geared to the accounting field.

Looking for a job is a job and should be treated as such. The more time you put into your job search, the shorter it will be. Conversely the less time you put into your job search the longer it may be. However, the most important thing is that you work smart and that you **"plan your work and work your plan"**. In doing so you will find the position you are searching for in as short a time as possible.

The Internet for Learning – Formal Education and Learning More Marketable Skills

The following section of the handbook is applicable whether you are choosing to stay in the job market and/or decide to run your own business. There is a wealth of learning on the internet, some as pricey as a college education and other education, training, and skills online learning, surprisingly affordable and some even free! For the sake of having common definitions is this section: Online EDUCATION program is defined here as online learning leading to a formal degree (Associate, Bachelors. Masters, etc.). While online TRAINING program would be leading to a Certificate type program. And online SKILLS program would give the user skills they did not have before taking the class, like individual computer coding classes, individual web design classes, etc.

The internet has opened up the entire world to learning in a whole new way. One does not need to go to "brick and mortar" class room any longer, can learn in the comfort of their home and learn as much as and fast as a person can take themselves. With that said, you can stay in the work place while learning at home to further your career in the market place. You can learn to run your own business or you can have a job and run your own business. You can learn how to do all of this and more from the internet. You can become, if you choose, a "One Person Industry". It is all available at your fingertips!

In the section of this handbook called RESOURCES (in the back of the handbook), there is a subsection called **Internet Based Education and Training**, where you will find a listing of websites that have companies specializing in any type of online learning you are interested in pursuing. From formal EDUCATION Programs, TRAINING Programs as well additional SKILLS training. Below is a listing of the online training vendors I have and continue to use:

1. **DigitalMarketer**: Digital Marketing Skills –
   www.DigitalMarketer.com

2. **Wainwright Global: Institute of Professional Coaching:** Life Coaching training –
   www.LifeCoachTrainingOnline.com

3. **Udemy**: Online learning and teaching marketplace –
   www.Udemy.com

4. **Course Horse**: Discover and compare the best classes and courses in NYC, LA, Chicago, Nashville, Houston, Boston & DC. - **https://CourseHorse.com/nyc**

5. **Grow with Google**: Free training, tools, and resources to help you grow your skills, career, or business. - **https://Grow.Google/**

Whenever you have a question on anything in either your professional or personal life use the internet as one of your main resources to learn and grow your base of knowledge. While Google.com and YouTube.com may not be the be all and end of information - you will be the smarter, wiser, and more prepared when you have to deal with the subject matter that you are interested in pursuing.

Chapter 27

Yes, You Can Have a Job and Live Your Life Purpose

Your Job and Your Work

As we spoke about earlier, there is a difference between having a job and performing your true "work". Do you have to leave your job or not have a job to do your work? The answer is no, you can have a job and do your work. **The ultimate experience is to have a job that is your work.** There are many benefits to a job. Since we do live in a material world, to a greater degree, the fact is we do need money, security, and host of other things that a job provides you and your family a sense of security and stability. It is important to realize that you are not your job and many times a job is just a means to an end.

There are many people that have a job and do their work part-time or on the weekends or whenever time permits. The most important thing is to acknowledge and perform your true "work". Your work has been created especially for you and can only be done by you for your specific spiritual growth. So a job may be a means to do your work. In time, you may want to do your work full time and/or run your own business as a means of doing your work. There is no right or wrong way. There is only your way, whatever works for you. **The most important thing is that you do your true "work" in whatever manner works for you.** By doing your work, you are helping yourself, other people and humankind evolve to a better place and a higher vibration.

Also, your work may not be a job at all. It may mean being the best parent you can be. Being a parent is "work" in itself for many a child owes their ability to do their "work" through the help of their parent and/or parents.

NOTES

NOTES

Chapter 28

Should I be an Entrepreneur and Run My Own Business?

Running your own business can be the most rewarding experience of your life, the freedom to do whatever you want and whenever you want to do it. It can also be the worse experience of your life, consuming every aspect of your life and all your finances. **Being an entrepreneur is not for everyone and not for people that are not willing to do whatever it takes. Be prepared to do things you have never done before and perform uncomfortable tasks that need to be done in order to run a successful business.** It can also be the most rewarding aspect of your life, taking a concept from thought to creation and delivering your product and/or service. Having a positive impact on other people lives and making money doing so will make you feel like you have made a real difference in this world.

The Business Plan

In starting your own business or any major new business venture it makes good sense to get a clear understanding as to what you are getting yourself into, financially and other wise. The **Business Plan** is the tool to help and guide you as to how to get started in setting up and running a business. A business plan is a document that summarizes the operational and financial objectives of a business and contains the detailed plans and budgets showing how the objectives are to be realized. Because the business plan contains detailed financial projections, forecasts about your business's performance, and a strategic marketing and plan, it's an incredibly useful tool for business planning and usually required if you need to get any type of financing from a bank or other financial institutions.

While the purpose of this handbook is not to teach you how to set up and run a business, there are two examples of business plans so you can get a better understanding of setting up and running your own business. The first example is a business plan for a service related business and the second business plan is for a product related business. Sample business plans are from the **www.MyOwnBusiness.org** website.

Sample Business Plan

(Service Business Plan)

SMITH E-COMMERCE CONSULTING

MARY SMITH

June 27, 2020

Section 1: The Business Profile

Description of My Business

I plan to provide a complete service for the design, installation, and maintenance of E-commerce marketing functions for my retail clients. I intend to evaluate the success of each installation and follow up to make changes to improve the effectiveness of each site.

Targeted Market and Customers

My customers will be small businesses that can enhance their present sales by the utilization of E-commerce. Typical clients will require sites for the dual purpose of providing 24-hour information to customers as well as providing a purchasing venue. Potential clients are businesses in which E-commerce can provide additional incremental sales. The businesses will range widely: from restaurants to neighborhood drug stores.

Growth Trends In This Business

The market for my services is growing at an unprecedented rate. In 2004 and 2005, year-end holiday shopping increased 25% each year.

Can you document from trade sources the anticipated rate of growth of your industry? If industry sources are not available, you will need to give a logical explanation as to the trend and potential of your intended market. This segment will provide you and your backers with information as to whether your market is growing or shrinking.

Pricing Power

Initially, my pricing power will be limited by what other consults charge for their time. However, I expect my business to be built by favorable word-of-mouth and my services to command a somewhat higher schedule of rates than average. I therefore expect that my reputation will gain me a degree of pricing power. Another factor is if my type of services are rendered ineffectively, it can be very costly and of no value to a client. On the other hand, if done well (by myself) the services can be affordable and immensely valuable. By gaining this reputation, I expect to be well paid for my work.

Section 2: The Vision and the People

Through my work experience and my former moonlight business, I possess unique skills to provide specialized E-commerce services. Also, I have had a long-term desire to be in business full time for myself and to utilize this knowledge. I have worked with many hardware and software vendors and Web site designers. Utilizing the resources of these associates, I can demonstrate competency in all aspects of successful E-commerce implementation. I am passionately committed to my new business and have the realism to make inevitable hard choices.

Educational Credentials

My education includes: _____ grade school, graduation from _____ high school (class of _____).

My higher education includes a _____ degree earned in _____ at _____ University, _____ year.

In _____ school I participated in the following activities (student council, student body officer, sorority/fraternity, clubs, etc.) I have also taken the following courses and seminars: My Own Business Internet Course, _____, _____.

My hobbies are: _____

My ongoing education includes subscriptions to the following professional journals: Wall Street Journal, Plastics World, etc.

I belong to the following professional and service organizations: National Association of Importers, Rotary Club, etc.

Work Experience Related to My Intended Business

My work experience has been as follows:

    1995 – 1998: Position _____ at _____ Co. Describe your work responsibilities in detail: _____

    1998 – 2009 Position _____ at _____ Co. Describe your work responsibilities in detail: _____

Section 2: The Vision and the People

My work experience with _____ company mentioned above included responsibility for Web-site design, implementation and maintenance. I have included a list of work references and character references in Exhibit A, attached.

I belong to the following professional organizations: *National Association of E-commerce Designers*

My consulting service will require specialized knowledge in all aspects of implementing E-commerce sites for small businesses. I have been moonlighting in this activity for 2 years and have successfully executed contracts with 5 small businesses. (See Exhibit __ including references, attached). I feel that this background qualifies me to undertake this business on a full time basis.

Section 3: Communications

Computer and Communications Tools

My business equipment requirements consist primarily of computer and communications tools. I have all of the following resources in place:

Resource Requirements:

Communications

Enter a description of all communications equipment.

Telephones

Enter a description of all telephone equipment.

Facsimile

Enter a description of all fax equipment.

Computers

Enter a description of all computer equipment.

Internet

Enter a description of necessary Internet providers.

Section 4: Business Organization

Business Organization

The form of business organization:

Initially I will be starting up the operation of Smith E-Commerce Consulting as a proprietorship. At my business grows and at a time my attorney feels appropriate, I will begin operating as a Limited Liability Corporation.

My main focus will be on the creation of websites that are user and search engine friendly for on-line purchasing functions.

Section 5: Licenses Permits and Business Names

Due Diligence Procedures for Licenses, Permits and Business Name

DBA: Smith E-Commerce Consulting. My intellectual property lawyer, an important consultant since I will be creating intellectual property for my clients, will do a search and if possible register my DBA (Doing Business As) name and logo.

Zoning: My start-up will be as a home based business. I have been advised by the City Hall clerk's office that I will qualify as an approved home business. My future office premises will be in a commercially zoned office space.

Licenses: The licenses I will need at the local, state, and federal level include:

Local: Municipal Business License from City Hall.

State: A state identification number will be secured from the Board of Equalization.

Federal: A federal EIN number will be secured from the IRS

Trademark: My trademarks will include my logo (to be designed) and my DBA name.

Sellers Permit: While I will not be charging sales tax on my services, at a future time when I begin marketing Internet equipment, I will secure a sellers resale permit from the state board of equalization.

Section 6: Insurance

I plan to consult with insurance agent Dan Deductable, who has been recommended by my accountant. My insurance coverage will be maintained in a "package" type insurance policy tailored for small service business such as mine.

Section 7: Location And Leasing

The criteria for my future office space will include:

- Space requirements including growth

- Site analysis study if needed (attach)

- Demographic study if needed (attach)

- Lease check-off list (attach)

- Estimated occupancy cost as a % of sales

- Zoning and use approvals

Section 8: Accounting and Cashflow

Accounting

Attached as a separate exhibit is my starting balance sheet and projected income statements for the first six months to one year.

Cash Flow Planning

Attached is an exhibit of my first year's cash flow projecting including estimated sales, all costs and capital investments.

Following is a checklist of all expense items included in the cash flow projection.

Analysis of Costs

Since my service business will initially be essentially intellectual property and advice, my start-up costs will be based on my living expenses and costs related to set-up of Websites, maintenance and operation of my office equipment, communication and computer functions. However pricing will include overhead, general and administrative expenses as if I were operating out of leased premises.

Internal Controls

As a service provider, I will personally be the only person controlling expenses, accounting and check signing. But at no time in the future will I delegate the authority for large purchase orders or check signing.

Section 9: How I Will Finance The Business

Financing Strategy

Attached is a spreadsheet showing all of the sources of my start-up capital. The major part of my start-up costs will come from savings. I have saved some money every month since I was fifteen years old and this nest egg will be my major source of initial working capital and equipment. I have also maintained three credit cards with balances paid promptly each month. The use of these credit lines will be for reserve purposes only and provided there are sources of repayment for any use of the cards. For example, to tide me over during periods of outstanding receivables. Once I have three years of profitable earnings statements, I plan to seek a regular line of bank credit. At a future time when I will begin marketing Internet technology hardware and software along with my services, I will look to my vendors for credit and advertising assistance.

Section 10: E-Commerce

E-Commerce Plans

Since my business will be to deliver E-Commerce solutions to retail businesses, it will be important for my clients to have outstanding website functions, furnishing valuable information and user-friendly navigation. Marketing by work-of-mouth referrals will be initially the most single means of new business. Once my initial client's sites are live and successful, I plan to start making calls on larger clients, using my successful installations as references.

As backlog builds, I plan to build a team of outsourced vendors including programmers, website designers, search engine consultants and copy experts. Ultimately Smith Consulting will become a turn-key outsourced E-commerce department for major retail operators.

E-Commerce Budgeting

My initial costs will be living expenses, purchase of additional office supplies, computer equipment and communications devices which are outlined as follow:

E-Commerce Competition

My best competitors are individual I.T. experts who moonlight as website developers and individuals who practice full-time. I plan to project a full-time business-like entity that merchants can look to as an ongoing and primary resource for designing, installing and continually upgrading their Internet marketing of goods and services. By emphasizing my full-time commitment as a consulting professional, I intend to grow to ongoing contracts with major players of retail Internet marketing.

Section 11: Buying A Business Or Franchise

Looking into the future, I may find opportunities to grow by purchasing the consulting practices of other Website designers. For example, to become a national firm there may be designers in other major markets who have reasons to sell their businesses and whose acquisition could result in "Smith Consulting Group" becoming a major national resource for major chain retailers.

Before starting my practice at home I will have my consulting team in place including business lawyer, accountant and intellectual property lawyer.

Acquisition of other businesses in my field will require a formal due-diligence checklist to investigate all aspects of the purchase:

Sellers records to be inspected: Financial statements, income tax returns, sales backlog, cash deposit records, utility bills, accounts payable and receivable, backlog, financial comparisons of similar businesses, etc.

Inspections and approval of leases and contracts.

Appraisals, as appropriate.

If a franchise, interview with randomly selected franchisees.

Finance plan for acquisitions: include sources including seller financing.

Market conditions.

Value of goodwill.

Method of purchase: stock, assets, etc.

Section 12: Marketing

Marketing Plan

My initial marketing will be to spend four hours per day on sales calls to local merchants who are not engaged in E-commerce. I will take initial assignments at reduced fees in order to establish a growing portfolio of successful users. I feel that the time spend on personal calls will outperform other means of marketing. Also I plan to promote and conduct free seminars that are addressed to local business owners. From these seminars I would make follow-up calls to seek out clients. I may collaborate with my C.P.A. in the conduct of these seminars.

Advertising and Promotion Plans

My initial advertising budget will be limited to expenses connected with seminars including room expense, local newspaper advertising and other expenses connected with seminar programming.

Purchasing and Inventory Control

Since I will be dealing entirely with intellectual property, my expenses connected with inventory and problems associated with purchasing goods will be eliminated.

The Competition

As covered in Section 10 of this plan, my principal competitors will be either moonlight operators or established firms.

How I Plan to Take Advantage of Competitors Weak Points

My emphasis will be to remove myself from competition by furnishing ongoing marketing advice, equipment upgrades, and new market opportunities to clients. The goal will be to establish, in effect, an ongoing consulting services to my clients to keep them on the cutting edge of not only technology but in e-commerce marketing techniques. I will be collaborating with my team of advisors including C.P.A. and attorney to be furnishing ongoing business insights as well as pitfalls to avoid.

Section 13: Growth Program

Expansion

My objectives of growth will be to expand from local individual businesses to small chains and ultimately to the major e-commerce chains throughout the country. It will be important to stay focused on providing all aspects of E-commerce solutions but not become engaged in unrelated IT responsibilities. By keeping my focus on E-commerce, I can carve out a niche that overtime can become a huge consultancy while avoiding competing with the major players in the IT hardware and software fields.

Handling Major Problems

An important part of my planning includes how I plan to handle adverse business conditions. The greatest risk I face is a large drop off in sales which would impact future liquidity. Attached are two pro-forma (estimated) cash flows, one with a 25% reduction in forecasted sales and another with a 40% drop in sales. In each case it will require prompt reduction in costs to avoid loss of liquidity (running out of money). In this manner I will have a plan in place to handle future cyclical swings in my business. These two cash flows are attached as exhibits.

Section 14: International Trade

Due Diligence Procedures for International Trade

Export Counseling: I do not plan to operate out of my own country for the next five to ten years. But at some point I anticipate that Smith Consulting will be engaged by multinational firms that will require me to have specialized knowledge of international business. My first step at this point will be to retain legal counsel specializing in international transactions. My international trade advisor will need to assist me in outlining the following preparations.

Export Readiness: *Describe the economic reasons and justification for my plans.*

Outline the personnel, budget and procedures I plan to implement.

Agent/distributor Agreement: *Provide a draft of your agent/distributor agreement and the agents/distributors I are considering doing business with.*

Analysis of Competitive Considerations: *Explain the due diligence resources to be used in the evaluation opportunities including appropriateness of your business.*

Evaluation of Country Risk: *Explain the resources to be used in the evaluation of*

country risk (is the country in good standing?) including potential sources of financing.

Describe your plans *to insure protection of intellectual property rights.*

Describe marketing and advertising plans.

Evaluate potential problems *regarding product adaptation to standards and measurements.*

Describe the licensing requirements *for export of your services.*

Section 15: Managing Employees

I plan to use a payroll service provider from the initial start-up, even including the early times I will be working by myself. This cost can be delegated for less than it would cost me to be handling start-up payroll, payroll deductions, local state and federal withholdings. I have received three proposals and intend to use _____ company.

Before hiring my first employee or delegating services to outsourced suppliers, I will prepare job description for each responsibility.

I have attached a copy of the job application I plan to use which is a stand form available at my office supplier.

When I begin to hire employees, I strongly feel that there will need to be an ample package of benefits for my employees in order to avoid turnover due to larger firms having more generous plans. My plan will include paid vacations, full medical coverage for my employees (not their dependents) and the company contributing $_____ per year to a Simple IRA plan.

I plan to complete an employee handbook before hiring any employees.

My initial and ongoing training programs for employees are attached as an exhibit.

Since future payroll problems can include great legal risks, at the time of hiring the first employee I plan to retain an attorney whose practice is limited to labor law.

Section 16: Home Based Business Issues

1. Factors in Starting as a home based business:

    1. My previous experience qualifies for conducting my own consulting business.

    2. For me, a home based start is appropriate and will keep my costs down.

    3. I can fully utilize Internet and communications tools at home.

    4. My home based zoning and licensing have been approved.

    5. As a full-time home based business I can project a professional image as my larger competitors.

2. The Home Based Business Format

    At the very beginning I plan to start as a moonlighter (without quitting my job) then switch to full time business at home, and later in an office setting.

    My preparations before quitting my job include: (see check list in session)

3. Conflict of interest management

    Since I will initially be starting business at home while working at my present job, I plan to strictly avoid conflict-of-interest risks by compartmentalizing my business completely away from my job responsibilities.

4. Operating personnel

    I do not plan to use any other family members in the home based operation of Smith Consulting, except for help in marketing seminars. My high school son, however, is fascinated with the prospects of a family business and is hoping to learn the basics as I expand.

Sample Business Plan

(Product Business Plan)

WIDGET CORPORATION

JAMES JONES

June 27, 2020

Section 1: The Business Profile

Description of My Business

I plan to market a complete line of bathroom accessories including "squeezies", soap dishes, toothbrush holders, coat hooks, and towel bars. The product line will be designed in my home office and manufactured and packaged in China.

Targeted Market and Customers

My customers will be discount department store chains with good credit ratings and reputations for prompt-payment. These will include Albertson's, Costco, Fleming, Wal-Mart, K-Mart, Target, and selected others.

Growth Trends In This Business

The market for household bathroom accessories is growing as population grows and new household formations take place. This is especially true in expanding economies as the standards of living make further gains. Also household purchases are increasingly being made through large chain discount retailers which I plan to focus on serving.

Pricing Power

I will not initially enjoy pricing power in marketing Widget accessories. Discount chains will be primarily interested in price. In order to achieve lower costs than my larger competitors I plan to do the following: _____.

My ultimate goal is to build a line so unique and promote it so effectively that consumers will be willing to pay a premium. My long-term objective is to build a market that is not entirely based on price. My unique features will include: _____.

Section 2: The Vision and the People

The Vision

I have a long-term plan to be in business for myself and to utilize the specialized business knowledge I have gained. The business relationships I have developed include vendors, discount chain buyers and manufacturing resources. They are: _____,

_____, _____. (List and explain in detail how they will help you).

The reasons that I feel my plans are realistic are: _____. I am the right person to pursue this opportunity because: _____.

There are special market conditions that are favorable to my getting started at this time.

They are: _____.

The People

Work Experience Related To My intended Business

My work experience has been as follows:

1995 – 1998 Position_____ at _____Co. Describe your work

responsibilities in detail: _____

1998 – 2006 Product Manager at ABC Imports Co. Describe your work

responsibilities in detail: _____

I have included a list of work references and character references as Exhibit A

Section 2: The Vision and the People

I have personal contacts in Hong Kong and Singapore who are ready to assist in the design, production, and packaging of the WIDGET line. Two large discount chains have encouraged me to make presentations to them.

Personal Background and Education Credentials

EDUCATION CREDENTIALS:

My education includes: _____ grade school, graduation from _____ high school (class of ____).

My higher education includes a ____ degree earned in _____ at_____, _____ year.

In _____ school I participated in the following activities (student council, student body officer, sorority/fraternity, clubs, etc.) I have also taken the following courses and seminars: My Own Business Internet Course, _____, and _____.

My hobbies are: _____

My ongoing education includes subscriptions to the following professional journals: Wall Street Journal, Plastics World, Fortune Magazine, Business Week.

I belong to the following professional and service organizations: National Association of Importers, American Plastics Association, The International Chamber of Commerce.

Section 3: Communications

Computer and Communications Tools

I plan to take advantage of all the computer and communications tools presently available to establish myself on the same level playing field as my large competitors. Following are the tentative specifications and budget for this equipment.

Resource Requirements:

Communications

Enter a description of all communications equipment.

Enter a budget for all communications equipment.

Telephones

Enter a description of all telephone equipment.

Enter a budget for all telephone equipment.

Facsimile

Enter a description of all fax equipment.

Enter a budget for all fax equipment.

Computers

Enter a description of all computer equipment.

Enter a budget for all computer equipment.

Internet

Enter a description of necessary Internet providers.

Enter a budget for Internet access.

Section 4: Organization

Business Organization

I plan to form a corporation for my business. It is my intention to grow Widget into a large firm with international relationships. The initial and ongoing costs of operating as a corporation will be a necessary business expense. Also, since a properly run corporation will afford me some limits of liability, I feel this is the right form of business for me. I intend to depend on my attorney to handle all aspects of setting up the corporation and maintaining proper corporate records.

Professional Consultants

I feel it is important that my team of professional advisors be in place before I start in business. Here is a list of these professionals:

Attorney: Suzie Catchum

Accountant: Norman Numbers

Insurance Agent: Paul Premium

Banker: Douglas Deeppockets

E-commerce Consultant: Mary Smith

Other: _____

Other: _____

Section 5: Business Licenses and Permits

My due-diligence procedures for licenses, permits and business names will be as follows:

DBA: I plan to do business as Premier Widget Corporation.

Zoning: Initially I will be working out of my home. When a staff is required I plan to move to a C-1 office space with a short-term lease with options to extend and expand.

Licenses: Licenses will be secured from appropriate authorities:

Local permits: Working at home: City Clerk at City Hall

State licensing: An account will be set up with the State Board of Equalization for sales tax reporting.

Federal: No federal licensing will be required.

Trademark: My attorney is conducting a trademark search for Premier Widget Corporation. If available we will follow our attorney's instructions in protecting the name.

EIN: AN employer's identification number has bee secured from the IRS.

Sellers Permit: None are required at the present time.

Section 6: Insurance

I plan to use the services of Paul Premium, my insurance agent. My insurance policies and limits of coverage are as follows:

Mr. Premium will provide me with a tabulation of all policies and limits of liability.

The company will not be self-insurance on any insurable risks.

Worker's Compensation insurance will be available from State Fund Insurance when I hire the first employee.

Section 7: Location And Leasing

During my start-up phase of approximately 6-12 months, I plan to operate out of my home office. Once my business is established, my initial office requirement will be approximately 1,000 square feet with two private offices and a secretarial area. My office criteria will include:

1. Convenience to my home.

2. A short-term lease of 1 - 2 years with two 1-year options.

3. A lease provision that the landlord provide me expansion space as required with a kickout clause if expansion space is not available.

4. Office layout including tenant improvements provided by the landlord. See Exhibit "C".

5. Lawyer review of the lease.

6. Use of the Lease Check-off list that is attached as an exhibit.

The use of these location criteria will gain me experience in handling much larger leases for space in the relatively near future. Future growth plans include warehousing of merchandise. I will be incurring large lease obligations that will be carefully reviewed.

Location Criteria

- Space requirements
- Future requirements
- Site analysis study (when needed)
- Demographic study (when needed)
- Lease check-off list (when needed)
- Estimated occupancy cost as a % of sales
- Zoning and use approvals

Section 8: Accounting And Cash Flow

Accounting

My knowledge of accounting is: _____. (*If you are deficient in basic accounting knowledge, then state how you intend to gain this needed know-how.*)

My accountant: I plan to work with C.P.A. Norman Numbers.

Accounting and payroll software programs: I will be using the following systems: _____.

Method of accounting: I will use the accrual method of accounting since this is generally required by the Internal Revenue Service for businesses dealing with manufacturing and inventory.

Business records: I will keep Widget accounts and records separate from my personal records.

Tax issues: My accountant, Mr. Numbers, will help me set up records for payments of social security tax, estimated income tax payments, payroll taxes and state withholding and sales taxes. My federal employer identification number (FEIN) is: _____. My state identification number is: _____.

Quarterly returns: Taxes will be paid in the appropriate time frames. Mr. Numbers will help me set up resale permit records for reporting to my state franchise tax board.

Bank account reconciliation: Bank accounts will be reconciled on a monthly basis.

Balance sheet: Attached is a separate exhibit of my starting balance sheet. Included is a schedule of equipment and fixtures needed that will appear on my balance sheet.

Section 8: Accounting And Cash Flow

Income statements: Attached are my projected income statements for the first six months and one year.

Internal Controls

My accountant, Norman Numbers, is experienced in my type of business, which includes international trade. He will help me set up a system of internal controls to make sure that Widget Corporation will receive all of its' income without any of it being siphoned off by waste, fraud, dishonest employees or carelessness.

This will include an inventory policy including who can sign for goods and services and who controls the release of goods and services out the door. Included in the internal control policy will be the requirement that the only person authorized to sign purchase orders, make capital acquisitions and sign checks will be myself personally.

Cash Flow Planning

Attached is an exhibit of my one-year cash flow analysis including estimated sales, all costs and capital requirements. I have included a checklist of all expense items for input into my cash flow projections.

Analysis of Costs

Attached is an itemized cost-breakdown of each individual Widget product that will be in my initial line. My initial target mark-up will be _____ %.

Section 9: Financing

Financing Strategy

My requirements for start-up capital are as follows:

Attached is a list of expenses for which I will require either start-up capital or financing. These items include buying supplies, getting a computer, equipment and fixtures, tooling, travel expenses and start-up overhead expenses. These expenses are included in my monthly cash flow projection to indicate the ongoing requirements for cash.

My sources of financing for starting my business are indicated in the following spreadsheet. While I will not be depending on banks for financing, there will be other resources available to me such as leasing of equipment and fixtures, credit from suppliers, mortgage financing, etc. My referrals include the following helpful contacts to lending institutions: my accountant, the Small Business Administration, friends, relatives, etc.

I am prepared to make presentations to potential lenders. My presentation kit includes this business plan, my personal financial statement and personal tax returns. I will be prepared to be specific in my needs for financing, the payback program and my sources of repayment. I will furnish potential lenders a cash flow projection showing sources of repayments and I will be conservative in my forecasts. A portfolio of referrals will be prepared for the finance package.

Section 10: E-Commerce

E-Commerce Plans

A website focusing on business-to-business E-commerce will be an important tool in my overall marketing program. I plan to build and install the www.widgetcorp.com website, which I have already registered. This will permit my discount department store customers to have access to my product line and to order (and reorder) merchandise via this website. I plan to hire Mary Smith of Smith E-Commerce Consulting Company to design, install and maintain this site.

The features of the www.widgetcorp.com site will include:

- It will be easy to use with good navigational features and prompt loading.

- The site will provide useful content including detailed information about all items in my product line.

- Purchasing procedures on a B-to-B basis will be designed and implemented.

- I intend to use the site to generate client feedback to help improve every aspect of my product line, operation and business procedures.

E-Commerce Budgeting

The cost breakdown of implementing my e-commerce activities are as follows:

E-Commerce Competition

The use of business-to-business e-commerce has become standard in my industry and is an important marketing tool. It is my intention to maintain a website that will project the image of a fresh and dynamic resource to my customers. I plan to keep abreast of the website developments of my competitors and to constantly improve my site.

My best competitors utilize e-commerce as follows (provide details). My strategy to improve on these practices include: Describe here.

Section 11: Business Acquisitions Strategy

Due Diligence Procedures for Acquisitions

I may have opportunities to acquire businesses in the future. In order to position myself to investigate acquisitions intelligently, the following "due diligence" process will be adhered to.

I will use a team of experts to give specific advice on the various components of the acquisition:

- Attorney
- Accountant
- Banker
- Broker
- Equipment supplier
- Other business owners

The following information will be required:

1. Sellers records and verification of revenues

2. Current financial statements

3. Cash deposit records

4. Supplier bills

5. Financial comparisons of similar businesses

6. Other _____

Section 11: Business Acquisitions Strategy

Valuation analysis will include:

- Basis for valuation: appraisals, etc.

- Method of purchase: stock, assets, etc.

- If a franchise, interview with randomly selected franchisees

- Evaluation of predictable future earnings

- Status of seller's motivation to sell

- Sources of acquisition financing

- Inspection of seller's personal and business tax returns

- Evaluation of leases and contracts

- Quality of improvements

- Quality and size of inventory. Obsolete merchandise?

- Condition of receivables

- Status of payables

- Status of verified order backlog

- Evaluation of customer relationships and goodwill

- Evaluate government approvals and licenses

- Status of pending litigation

- Other _____

Section 12: Marketing

Marketing Plan

I plan to focus all initial marketing efforts on establishing a beachhead at one large discount department store chain. I will personally be responsible for the contacts with the appropriate buyers. My complete line will be presented as a package including display accessories that tie into the merchandising policies of each chain. Initially my price structure will be based on a maximum markup of _____% in order to provide a strong price incentive. I will be depending on the combination of fresh styling, quality and price to break into this market.

Advertising and Promotion Plans

Short Range Plan (6 to 12 months): Initially my advertising and promotion will be done on an entirely personal basis without any budget for paid advertising. My customers require personal visitation by the CEO's of their vendors. It will be my plan to limit my advertising budget to personal travel expenses in making these presentations and follow-up presentations.

Mid-Range Plan (12 – 36 months): To establish brand recognition at the retail level, I plan to budget _____% of my sales to joint advertising with my discount department store customers. I will solicit presentations from local advertising agencies.

Long Range Plan: I plan to aggressively build brand recognition and loyalty by budgeting _____% of sales, which will be allocated between space advertising in trade journals, appropriate consumer magazines and joint advertising with my customers.

Section 12: Marketing

Purchasing and Inventory Control

For replenishment of stocks I plan to participate in just-in-time tracking with my customers, utilizing their on-line business-to-business computer systems in place. As much as possible, warehousing will be kept to a minimum by use of direct and rapid delivery systems.

The following procedures will be implemented:

We will ask for 30-day payment terms and offer 2% discount for 10 days.

An inventory control system will be maintained.

All merchandise received will be counted and inspected.

We will pay our contractors on time and be loyal to them.

We will ask for and take term discounts.

Purchase Orders will include:

    Price and terms

    Price protection

Always in writing:

    Complete specifications

    Delivery deadlines

    All promises will be verified in writing

    Appropriate contingencies will be included in purchase orders

    Any changes or extras must have prior approval in writing

Internal controls will be in place for shipping and receiving

Section 12: Marketing

The Competition

My principal competitor is Colossal Plastics Company. I have included a list of all major competitors in this business and a brief sketch including to whom they sell. (Provide a tabulation of these competitors).

How I Plan to Take Advantage of my Competitors Weak Points

My biggest competitor is Colossal Plastics Company, which has a 20-year history of success and has gained strong brand-recognition. But they have developed a large overhead structure, which I will not have. They are also slow to make changes and upgrades to their line of products. I plan to overcome their leadership with fresh new designs, artwork and attractive packaging and to be priced very competitively. I intend to continually introduce additions and refinements to the line.

Also, my end-user profile is for younger families who are not impressed by old-line brand names. Operating with a very low overhead, I believe I can gain a foothold in this market. A similar profile of my other principal competitors is enclosed indicating their weak spots and how I plan to capitalize on these deficiencies.

Section 13: Growth program

Expansion Plans

Once my business has been established I plan to implement the following growth strategy. I anticipate it will take approximately _____ (months or years) to gain sufficient experience and level of profits before any expansion plans are implemented.

My growth strategy will be guided by the following:

I will not set an inflexible timetable for expansion but will wait until a sound basis of experience, earnings and cash flow is achieved. (If you intend to expand as a chain of stores or units, here's where you should take a stand to say that your initial pilot operation will be on a sound earnings basis before you begin to add more units.)

Accounting and cash flow controls will be in place with profit and loss statements prepared for individual expansion units on a _____ (monthly, etc) basis.

Internal controls for accounting, money handling and inventory will be in place.

My attorney will review all documentation regarding expansion. This will include leases, employment and incentive agreements, licensing and franchise agreements, important commitments with vendors and customers, etc.

It is my intention that expansion plans will not change my policy of taking adequate time for my family.

Hiring and training policies will be in place. Fringe benefit plans will be in place.

Section 13: Growth program

My intention is to delegate authority and responsibility to expansion management personnel with the following conditions in place:

1. Managers will be motivated by a profit incentive plan that will be tied to manager's individual success. My plan will be in writing, simply stated and will call for frequent periods of accountability. A sample of my manager's incentive compensation plan is attached.

2. Capital allocations and signing checks will not be delegated.

3. I intend to maintain an ongoing study of my competitors. Their successes and failures will help me form guidelines on what to do and not to do.

I plan to development profitable pilot operations before undertaking full-scale production. Analysis will be made of sources of financing, cash flow, accounting systems, incentive compensation plans for managers, and economics of scale.

Handling Major Problems

My policy in handling problems will be to identify and acknowledge problems promptly and honestly. I plan to put the following policies into effect promptly if the following adverse scenarios emerge during my growth program:

The risk of running out of cash: I plan to maintain very frequent (_____monthly?) cash flow projections. Forecasts for income, expenses and unanticipated contingencies will be stated conservatively. Any periods of cash deficits will be remedied promptly by cutting costs to maintain a positive cash flow and profitability.

Section 13: Growth program

A drop in sales or insufficient sales:

1. I will be prepared to take prompt remedial steps by cutting costs.

2. I will improve every aspect of product value, performance and image

3. I will seek out new ways to expand sales by _____.

4. I plan to stick with this specialized business that I know best unless fatally defective.

Dishonesty, theft, and shrinkage: I intend to implement the same policies that have been proven by _____ company, one of my biggest competitors.

Business recessions: I am prepared to promptly cut costs to maintain liquidity. I will also be on the lookout for good business opportunities during periods of adversity. Scenarios of adverse conditions will be prepared and solutions on how I intend to respond to them included. Included in this analysis will be projected cash flow projections based on a 25% and 45% reduction in sales. The main objective will be to promptly initiate cost reductions in order to preserve ongoing liquidity.

Section 14: International Trade

Due Diligence Procedures for International Trade

Export Counseling: My team of counselors will include a consultant or lawyer who specializes in international trade. All documentation will be approved by this consultant.

Export Readiness: International trade will become a key part of my success because of the dependency on importing my precision molded products. This dependence is based on cost advantages of imported goods. Initially, I will personally be responsible for all transactions.

Agent/distributor Agreement: A draft of my agent/distributor agreement (prepared by; my consultant) and the agents/distributors I am considering to do business with is attached.

Analysis of Competitive Considerations: I will retain my consultant to initially perform the due diligence on evaluating opportunities.

Evaluation of Country Risk: I will participate in the study of resources to be evaluated and potential country risk, including potential sources of financing.

Protection of intellectual property rights: My intellectual property lawyer will be responsible for handling intellectual property diligence in protection of my names, products and trade secrets.

Marketing: My marketing and advertising plans will emphasize the low price/high value nature of Widget products for sale through large discount retailers.

Standards and measurements: Potential problems regarding product adaptation to standards and measurements will be vetted and resolved where necessary.

Licenses: Our international consultant will determine all licensing requirements for export and/or import of our products. I plan to market Widget products throughout the world.

Section 15: Managing Employees

Training Policies

Initially I will personally handle sales to my discount department store customers. As my business expands, I intend to begin marketing to smaller retailers. I will hire sales associates who can gain the confidence of smaller buyers who want to deal with vendors that are knowledgeable and helpful. To achieve these qualities I will look for the following characteristics in marketing employees. People who:

- Like what they do

- Are quick learners

- Project a pleasant and positive image

- Like people and relate well to them

- Are helpful to customers and fellow associates

- Are ambitious and seek to grow in responsibilities

I will follow a checklist in hiring marketing associates:

- Have a hiring policy in place including written salary structure, commission compensation and perks

- Create job descriptions for everyone

- Conduct ongoing marketing meetings

- Have written policies and procedures on handling customer complaints

- Maintain clear guidelines for pricing policies and handling customer's inquiries

Section 15: Managing Employees

I plan to outsource the handling of payroll and payroll accounting and reporting to XYZ Services Company.

I have included copies of job descriptions for all employees I will be hiring during the first year.

Attached is a copy of the job application form and screening procedures I intend to use. Screening procedures will include drug testing, criminal records, checks with prior employers and proficiency at the job skills required.

Our benefits package will include 100% health coverage for employees but not for dependents. Three percent of annual wages will be contributed by the company toward employee's Simple IRA retirement plans. Vacation will be paid for up to two weeks per year.

Attached is a copy of my intended employee handbook.

Initial and ongoing training programs for employees will be mandatory and at company expense.

Labor attorney Mr/Ms ._____will be advising me on employee matters.

Section 16: Home Based Business

Factors in Selecting Home Based

1. I have had 15 years background in precision molded plastics plus marketing experience to chain store purchasing departments.

2. I will be starting Widget Corporation at home in order to conserve cash during the getting ready period.

3. The intensive use of Internet technology which I will deploy can be handled from my home base as well.

4. My home is zoned for a home based business such as the office requirements of Widget.

My Home Based Business Format

I will first start as a moonlighter, while keeping my regular job, and then when appropriate switch to full-time at home, and finally to operation out of suitable office quarters.

Conflict of Interest Management

During the initial period when I will be operating as a moonlighter (while still holding my job) I will observe all necessary measures to compartmentalize Widget away from my employment as well as avoidance of any conflict possibilities.

Operating Personnel While Operating from Home

During the home-based period of Widget, both my wife and our two high school sons will be acting is supportive roles: My wife handling accounting and website development and my sons helping with Internet researching of potential vendors.

The Marketing and Sales Strategic Plan

The next plan to discuss, which may seem even more important and a subset to the Business Plan is the **Strategic Marketing and Sales Plan**.

The Strategic Marketing and Sales Plan are the specific details, who, what, when, where and how you will be marketing and selling your products and/or service. **Marketing and Selling are two different functions of your business.** Though they are interdependent upon one another, they need to be understood and planned for accordingly.

On the next pages is a sample **Strategic Marketing and Sales Plan** and an exercise to write your own.

Sample Strategic Marketing and Sales Plan

Your Strategic Marketing and Sales Plan

Your Strategic Marketing and Sales plan (a subset of your main business plan), also known as your Marketing and Sales plan, is a road map for how you are going to market and sell your products and/or services into the market place and by doing so make money. The strategic marketing and sales plan discussed here is a simple one, but it will help you organize your thoughts as to what you are going to do and how you are going to do it.

There is no "one way" to write a strategic marketing and sales plan and there are many books on the subject. This Strategic Marketing and Sales Plan (not the same one as in the previous examples) will get you started immediately to organize your thoughts, be productive as soon as possible and by doing so start generating revenues (money) as quickly as possible.

First, we will discuss the components of the strategic marketing and sales plan. Then you will see an outline of a marketing and sales plan and a sample marketing and sales plan. In addition, you have some worksheets where you can write your own marketing and sales plan.

When writing your marketing and sales plan remember to keep things simple and easy. It only needs to be a few pages as you can always go back and adjust things later. This is a "living document" and you will change things as you see what works and doesn't work.

Components of a Marketing and Sales Plan

1. Mission Statement - In order to write your mission statement, you need to be able to answer the following: Why should this business exist? Who will be its customers and how will it benefit them? Why will they be better off after purchasing your product or service?

2. Business Objective(s) – What do you want to accomplish with your business? (make money for your self and family, give people jobs, etc.)

3. Target Market(s) – To whom specifically do you want to sell your product and/or service? The more precise the target, the more business you will close.

4. Marketing Strategies – How are you going to market and sell to your target market? (Summary Level – Ex.: Advertising then in Marketing activities define the day-to-day details – Local Newspapers, Digital Marketing, etc.)

5. Marketing Activities – What are the day-to-day activities you are going to pursue to get your name out in the market place (e.g. Business Networking, Trade Shows, Advertising, etc.)?

6. Goals – What are your weekly, monthly, and quarterly goals in the areas of making appointments, closing deals, revenues, etc.?

7. Territory – What is the geographic span of your business? Is it local towns, the state, the region, the country, or the world?

8. Administration – How will you be tracking and maintaining all aspects of your business?

Marketing and Sales Plan Outline

1. Mission Statement

2. Business Objectives (s)

3. Target Market(s)

4. Marketing Strategies (Summary)

5. Marketing Activities (Detail – Day to Day Activities)

6. Goals

    - Weekly Goals

    - Monthly Goals

    - Quarterly Goals

7. Territory

8. Administration

Last Update: January 20, 2020

SAMPLE MARKETING AND SALES PLAN

(For a sales person in a business. Concepts are the same if you are writing it for yourself as a business owner.)

Acme Consulting Inc.

2020 Strategic Marketing Sales Plan
for John Smith

1. Mission Statement

To provide Acme Consulting, business partners, prospective, and current clients with excellence of sales and service in the area of integrated business solutions (consulting, coaching and training services) for human resources.

2. Business Objective (s)

The objective of this plan is to make Acme Consulting the leading provider of integrated business solutions for the SAP (computer software for companies) marketplace in the northeast region of the United States by increasing market share of Acme Consulting integrated business solutions.

3. Target Market (s)

The target market will be the SAP Human Resources marketplace in the **N**ortheast United States, specifically, companies who have purchased or are looking to purchase SAP Human Resources software solutions.

4. Strategies

The strategy I will use to close business and to separate myself from other vendors is to use a "consultative sales approach" method when dealing with prospective and current clients. In addition, when qualifying prospects, and in my initial meetings and presentations, I will use the F.I.N.D. (Facts, Issues, Needs, Dreams) Sale Methodology. This sales approach stresses the concept of "value add" when providing integrated services and will have the prospect view Acme Consulting as a "business partner" rather than just another business solutions vendor in the market place.

5. Marketing Activities

- Targeted mailing to SAP customers in the northeast with telephone follow up. All mailings should be followed up with a phone call to ensure information has been received and all business contacts at that location are explored.

- Call SAP sales and delivery representatives approximately twice each month to monitor any opportunities that SAP is working on where Acme Consulting can bring value.

- Follow up on all leads furnished by the various Acme Consulting corporate departments. Follow up to be performed on a timely basis as to get prospects while their interest is at its peak. Continue telemarketing of said leads to ensure all leads are monitored properly.

- Attend and participate in all appropriate networking and opportunities with SAP sales and delivery representatives.

6. Goals

Weekly Goals

- **Two (2)** appointments/presentations per week with prospects.

- **One (1)** meeting/strategic phone call with SAP sales and/or delivery representatives.

- **One (1)** meeting/strategic phone call with current clients with the goals of keeping client satisfaction high and to gain client as a reference.

- Prospect for new leads and follow-up on existing leads.

- Keep current on status of suspects, prospects and clients.

- Check on and move deals down "pipeline".

- Work on presentation skills. Increase services knowledge.

Monthly Goals

- **Eight (8)** appointments/presentations per week with prospects.

- **Four (4)** meetings/strategic phone calls with SAP sales and/or delivery representatives.

- **Four (4)** meetings/strategic phone calls with current clients with the goals of keeping client satisfaction high and to gain client as a reference.

- Prospect for new leads and follow-up on existing leads.

- Keep current on status of suspects, prospects and clients.

- Check on and move deals down "pipeline".

- Work on presentation skills. Increase services knowledge.

Quarterly Goals

- **Twenty Four (24)** appointments/presentations per week with prospects.

- **Twelve (12)** meetings/strategic phone calls with SAP sales and/or delivery representatives.

- **Twelve (12)** meetings/strategic phone calls with current clients with the goals of keeping client satisfaction high and to gain client as a reference.

- Prospect for new leads and follow-up on existing leads.

- Keep current on status of suspects, prospects and clients.

- Check on and move deals down "pipeline".

- Work on presentation skills. Increase services knowledge.

7. Territory

The territory for this position consists of the Northeast Region of the United States, specifically the following states: Maine, Vermont, New Hampshire, Massachusetts, Connecticut, New York, New Jersey, Pennsylvania, and Maryland.

8. Administration

The administration of information is critical to ensure the activities mentioned are carried out and monitored properly. I will be timely in all reports, preparation, and delivery of all proposals to prospects, clients and other necessary written and verbal requirements to the management team. I will learn and use ACT contact management software to manage my time and territory in an efficient and productive manner.

Last updated 01/28/2020 at 2:00pm

Exercise: Pros and Cons of Running Your Own Business

- Spend some time reading and writing the Business Plan and the Strategic Marketing and Sales Plan. Have them reviewed by **SCORE** (SCORE.org – they have a library of templates like business plans and other templates) **America's premier source of free business mentoring and education**, a resource partner of the U.S. Small Business Administration (SBA), SCORE has helped more than 11 million entrepreneurs through mentoring, workshops, and educational resources since 1964. Then have your attorney and accountant review your business plans as well.

- Then make a list of the "Pros" and "Cons" of starting and running your own business. This exercise will help you get clarity if running a business is right for you. This exercise is not designed to dissuade (not to take a particular course of action) you into not starting your own business, but rather meant to give you a "reality check" as what it takes to be successful.

NOTES

Chapter 29

Business Tools to Help You with Your Business

Use Different Tools for Different Tasks –
When You only have a Hammer
every Problem Looks like a Nail!

Running your own business is going to require you to have different tools in your "Business Tool Kit" to do different business tasks to operate a successful business. If you are a "task oriented" person, then you are going to need "people skills." Conversely, if you are a people oriented person, you are going to need the disciple of doing tasks, processes, and procedures. While you can outsource some of the things you don't like to do or can't do, remember, the more you outsource business tasks, the less profit you are going to make. You don't need to be a master at everything, but a "jack of all trades" mentality certainly does help when running your own business. Running your own business does require you to have an open mind about learning new things. The more you can do for yourself, the more savings in time and money you will achieve for your business in the long run. I never thought I would be writing books, let alone having my articles appear in trade magazines, and being on radio and even television. I taught myself how to do this, by reading books on the subjects, observing what others like me did and asking questions. You can do all this as well. It will take a bit of an investment of time and some money, but you will use these new skills the rest of your professional life in and out of your business.

Embrace Technology

Technology is here to stay and will be a very important part of your business. You do not need to become a "tech head" but you do need to have a fundamental understanding and working knowledge of technology, what it does and how it can expand your business productivity and profitability. Technology has come a long way since I went to technical school learning to punch IBM computer cards, to the modern day, where mobile phones are mobile computers with a telephone attached.

If you are not technology savvy, start off by going to Google (www.Google.com) and research and download a "Glossary of Computer Terms". This is an excellent starting point to get you familiar with terms and phrases in computing and technology. As mentioned in a previous chapter, Google has a wealth of technology training free of charge. Next, take class(es) at a local high school and/or college continuing education program. There is no ONE class title that you can learn everything you need to know technology wise to run a business. Technology has become like the medical field where everything has become a specialty. Do as much technology stuff as you can handle and like to do. Outsource the really difficult things but know enough about the technology and what needs to be done so you can have an intelligent conversation with the technical person you are outsourcing to do the work.

Work Smart: Task and Self-Management

Working smart is the name of the game. What does working smart really mean? It means working as intelligently as possible, to be very productive, make as much money as you can and lose as little money as possible while doing so. Running a business requires discipline. Discipline in performing tasks, discipline in yourself and discipline in managing time. You will find that your business life will become a series of **MBOs** (Management By Objectives). Things need to get done and you are the person to do them. So every working day, get up and set for yourself a MANAGEABLE list of things to get done in and for your business. I say "manageable" because manageable helps prime the engine of success! You write twelve business tasks to do today and only 3 get done. How does that make you feel? How about writing six business things to do today and get them ALL done! Now how does that make you feel? ☺ Slow and steady wins the race in business. Take "calculated risks" and not "gambles" when necessary to move ahead and even catapult your business.

Time and Money, Money and Time the Zen of Managing Both

We've all heard the expression "time is money." It has never been as true as when you work for yourself. Every time you make a business decision (and you will be making them daily) you must think about the amount of time it will take and the amount of money you will either be making or losing to do that task. Now keep in mind that you do have to make investments in time and money to further your business. Th**e challenge is to make MORE <u>RIGHT</u> decisions than WRONG decisions**. It is an art and science that every business owner hopes to learn and master. The better you get at it the more successful you, your business will be and the more money you will make.

Time Management Tools

When running your own business, it's important to develop the discipline of time management. And yes, it is a discipline. In the beginning of any business venture there is much to be done. All of us have the same number of hours in the day and days in the week, etc. The trick is to work as productively as possible within these hours. As previously mentioned, you will find that your business life becomes life by **MBOs** (Management by Objectives). Things need to get done and you have to do them (until you start making enough money to hire employees, then you can delegate some things to them).

You need to be mindful of the **"Money Hours"** of your business. The Money Hours are the time of each business day in which money is to be made, collected, paid, etc. During these hours, your focus should be on getting money (deals), moving deals along, working with customers and servicing customers. During the Money Hours you are not stuffing envelopes, going to the store, watching television, etc. With that said your money hours, for example, may be from 8:00am to 11:30am in the morning and 1:30pm and 4:30pm in the afternoon. So by using proper time management you can stuff envelopes, go to the store, watch television, etc., before the Money Hours start, at lunchtime and after the Money Hours are over. This time management discipline is a very good habit to get into to so you can be as productive as possible without "burning out."

Below are two-time management tools to get you started. Find the system you like or create your own. All successful people use some sort of time management system to get things done in their world and you should too. Others time management tools can be found at **www.MindTools.com**.

I have also included some other business tools in this section that you will need and/or may grow into as the need arises. Do not be intimidated by all these tools and this information. Some you will use immediately, while others will be used at a later date or you will grow into them as your business expands.

The One-Percent Solution*

(Time Management Tool)

- Unless you manage your time you will not be able to manage anything else. The management of your time is the foundation for your effectiveness. (Drucker, 2006, page 11).

Four Facts About Time:

Fact One: Time is a Limited Resource

Fact Two: Time is an Inflexible Resource

Fact Three: There will Always be More Things to do Than Time to do them

Fact Four: Focus, not Efficiency, is the Key to Mastering our Time

The following is a very simple system that allows you to apply the above principles

- Devote 30 minutes one time each week to access the past week and plan the next week

- Identify **four to six** areas of your life, both personally and professionally, that are your highest priorities.

- Target one or two of the most important steps of action to be accomplished this week for each priority area.

- Schedule your top priority steps of action first in your calendar for the week.

- Devote **five minutes** each day to adjust your schedule and realign with your priorities.

- **Use the A, B, C, D, E Priority Method**

    - **A Task:** Top Priority

    - **B Task**: Needs to be done this week

    - **C Task:** Low Priority to be done by month's end

    - **D Task:** Delegate to Someone Else

    - **E Task:** Eliminate or do not do the task

EXAMPLE

The Weekly Planning Worksheet

PRIORITIES	THIS WEEK'S STEPS OF ACTION
Area One Myself	- Exercise five times this week; M/T/W/Th/Sat. - Make an appointment to see my doctor.
Area Two My Family	- Take my wife/husband/partner out to dinner on Friday. - Get a sitter. - Plan a family trip to the zoo.
Area Three Recruit Top Talent	- Set up interviews with top candidates.
Area Four Rehire My Best People Every Day	- Place birthdays of team members in my calendar. - Purchase personalized thank you cards for quick notes to team members. Write two.
Area Five Build Internal Relationships	- Contact HR department head and schedule her/him to come in and speak to our team.
Area Six Excel at Coaching Team Members	- Schedule one-on-one review sessions with each team member for the next month. - Conduct one hour-long review session this week.

© 2007 Leadership Link, Inc.

* Fairley, Stephen, G and Zipp, William. **The Business Coaching Toolkit: Top 10 Strategies for Solving the Toughest Dilemmas Facing Organizations**. Hoboken, NJ: John Wiley & Sons, 2007.

The Weekly Planning Worksheet

PRIORITIES	THIS WEEK'S STEPS OF ACTION
Area One	
Area Two	
Area Three	
Area Four	
Area Five	
Area Six	

© 2007 Leadership Link, Inc.

SAMPLE - To Do List

Things TO DO Today

Date: _____   Completed Y/N:

1. _____   _____
2. _____   _____
3. _____   _____
4. _____   _____
5. _____   _____
6. _____   _____
7. _____   _____
8. _____   _____
9. _____   _____
10. _____   _____
11. _____   _____
12. _____   _____
13. _____   _____
14. _____   _____
15. _____   _____
16. _____   _____

Hint for Success: Only place on this list the things you can **REALISTICALLY** get done each day, so you earn a sense of accomplishment when completed.

Goal Setting

Goal setting is a powerful process for thinking about your ideal future, both in your professional and your personal life, as well as for motivating yourself to turn your vision of this future into reality. The process of setting goals helps you choose where you want to go in your world.

Below is a sample methodology for setting business goals. Use it or find one that you like and implement it. Goal setting will help give you clarity of mind to get where you want to go.

Business Coaching Exercise:

Making Goals S-M-A-R-T*
A Business Case for Better Goals

Goals don't work for the following reasons:

- Goals by Themselves Do Not Provide Context

- Context is critical to Goal setting.

- A goal that is set without understanding the bigger picture of overall business objectives and fundamental priorities can ruin the organization.

- Goals Alone Do Not Bring Fulfillment

- A **goal** gives us the _**how**_, but without a greater _**why**_ we lose our energy and endurance. With a _**how**_ we have a job; with a _**why**_ we have a cause. A **cause** is what ignites our passion and empowers us to act.

- All goals need a **context**, the overall strategy in which they function, and a cause. There must be a set of underlying values it seeks to serve, a deeper _**why**_ to sustain the _**how**_. Goals alone do not supply these and do not work without them.

Better Goals are S-M-A-R-T Goals

S – Be Specific

First, a S-M-A-R-T goal is **SPECIFIC**. It says exactly what you want to do in clear, concrete terms. This is the fundamental difference between a wish and a goal. Wishes get us nowhere in business, but you would be surprised how many leaders fail at this first, fundamental point. While making a goal, S-M-A-R-T forces us to ask, "What is it exactly you want to do?" If the answer is, "I want to increase sales," this is not a goal; it is a wish. "I want a more positive work environment," also fails the S-M-A-R-T test. But if you said, "I want to reduce employee turnover by 25 percent," you now have the beginnings of a S-M-A-R-T goal.

M – Be Measurable

Second, a S-M-A-R-T goal is **MEASURABLE**. Measurement is often inherent in the specifics of the goal, but not always. You may want to increase customer satisfaction but have no way of measuring it. A survey might work, a focus group, or even increased sales. To be S-M-A-R-T, a goal must land on means of measuring success and be trackable over time.

A – Be Achievable

Our goals must stretch us, yes, but the stretch must be reasonable, balanced with other priorities and be **ACHIEVABLE**. Talk with others about the feasibility of your goals. Look at industry standards and reflect on the accomplishments of those who have gone before you.

R – Be **Relevant**

RELEVANT goals must be in line with overall business objectives.

Relevance is the key to sustained goal fulfillment. We won't accomplish something over time that we are not internally committed to with all our heart. Again, goals are our servants, not our masters, and must serve the greater purpose of our values and priorities to truly be S-M-A-R-T.

T – Be **Time** Bound

Finally, if you don't have a deadline (a specific **TIME**), you don't have a goal. The specifics of the goal must answer the question, "By when?" Intermediate time targets, called milestones, can also be set for your goal. Milestones keep a person on track with reasonable progress toward the finish line.

Business Coaching Exercise
The S-M-A-R-T Goal Worksheet

Here is a five-step system for setting goals that work.

1. State Your Goal in One Sentence and Make it **S-M-A-R-T**

2. List the Main Benefits of Achieving This Goal

3. List the Steps of Action for Achieving This Goal

4. List the Possible Obstacles for the Completion of This Goal

5. List the Possible Solutions to the Obstacles of This Goal

S-M-A-R-T GOAL WORKSHEET

Name: John Jones	**Date:** Feb. 2, 2020

S-M-A-R-T Goal (Specific, Measurable, Relevant, Time bound)
To achieve $1.8 million of agricultural sales in 2007 by selling $600K of fertilizer by April, $600K of fungicide and growth regulator by June, and $600K of lime, herbicide, and other products by December.
BENEFITS of Achieving this Goal
I will feel a great sense of accomplishment of having sold more product than in any other year.
I will feel good about the job I am doing for my company; a place where I enjoy working.
I will enjoy increased pay through commissions and bonuses.
I will set the table for years of repeat business with these customers.
STEPS of ACTION for Achieving this Goal
1. Update and analyze soil samples of all my customers by February 24.
2. Write up fertilizer blend recommendations based on soil samples by March 8.
3. Make appointments with all my customers to present recommendations by March 10.
4. Apply first round of dry fertilizer by March 30.
5. Apply second round of liquid fertilizer by April 30.

Possible OBSTACLES	Possible SOLUTIONS
1. Letting a bottleneck develop by doing all of my own soil sample work.	1. Work closely with scouts to help with gathering soil samples.
2. Losing sales due to pricing concerns.	2. Get pricing strategy set before customers bring it up.
3. Losing sales due to product supply.	3. Solve the problem at management level.

How Many S-M-A-R-T Goals Should a Person Work on at One Time?

How many goals should you have? Less is more. I recommended focusing on two, at the most three, S-M-A-R-T goals at one time. Beyond that I have observed that a person gets overwhelmed and performance diminish.

GOAL WORKSHEET

Name:	Date:

S-M-A-R-T Goal (Specific, Measurable, Relevant, Time bound)

BENEFITS of Achieving this Goal

STEPS of ACTION for Achieving this Goal

Possible OBSTACLES	Possible SOLUTIONS

*Fairley, Stephen, G and Zipp, William. **The Business Coaching Toolkit: Top 10 Strategies for Solving the Toughest Dilemmas Facing Organizations**. Hoboken, NJ: John Wiley & Sons, 2007.

How to Make Decisions
- Decision Making Tools from www.MindTools.com

How to Make Decisions

All of us have to make decisions every day.

Some decisions, like, "Is this report ready to send to my boss now?" are relatively straightforward and simple. While others, such as, "Which of these candidates should I select for the job?" can be quite complex.

Simple decisions usually need a simple decision-making process. But difficult decisions typically involve issues like these:

- **Uncertainty** – Many facts may not be known.

- **Complexity** – You have to consider many interrelated factors.

- **High-risk consequences** – The impact of the decision may be significant.

- **Alternatives** – Each has its own set of uncertainties and consequences.

- **Interpersonal issues** – It can be difficult to predict how other people will react.

With these difficulties in mind, the best way to make a complex decision is to use an effective process. Clear processes usually lead to consistent, high-quality results, and they can improve the quality of almost everything we do. In this article, we outline a process that will help improve the quality of your decisions.

A Systematic Approach to Decision Making

A logical and systematic decision-making process helps you address the critical elements that result in a good decision. By taking an organized approach, you're less likely to miss important factors, and you can build on the approach to make your decisions better and better.

There are six steps to making an effective decision:

1. Create a constructive environment.
2. Generate good alternatives.
3. Explore these alternatives.
4. Choose the best alternative.
5. Check your decision.
6. Communicate your decision and take action.

Key Points

An organized and systematic decision-making process usually leads to better decisions. Without a well-defined process, you risk making decisions that are based on insufficient information and analysis. Many variables affect the final impact of your decision. However, if you establish strong foundations for decision making, generate good alternatives, evaluate these alternatives rigorously, and then check your decision-making process, you will improve the quality of your decisions.

Problem Solving

Whether you're *solving* a *problem* for a customer, supporting those who are *solving problems*, or discovering new *problems* to *solve*, the *problems* you face can be large or small, simple, or complex, and easy or difficult. A fundamental part of every business is finding ways to *solve* them.

Some problems are easy to solve, and some are more complex and complicated to solve. Below is a business industry standard method to solve more sophisticated problems. If your problem is big enough, it may merit a **S-W-O-T Analysis.** Again, don't be overwhelmed by this information, use it if you need it, but I suspect as your business grows, you will have a problem that will warrant this type of analysis.

S-W-O-T Analysis *

S-W-O-T stands for **S**trengths, **W**eaknesses, **O**pportunities and **T**hreats. It is a way of summarizing the current state of a company and helping to devise a plan for the future, one that employs the existing strengths, redresses existing weaknesses, exploits, opportunities and defends against threats.

A New Twist on S-W-O-T

	Internal Reality	External Reality
Positive	Strengths	Opportunities
Negative	Weaknesses	Threats

Below is a sample of a **S-W-O-T** analysis in action. Change the questions to the problem you are experiencing at the time. The questions don't have to be complicated or sophisticated just a means to expose as many issues as possible before you make a business decision.

Strengths

1. What do clients and outside partners say is your top strength?

2. What do you currently do better than anyone else?

3. What were your motivating factors and influences in starting this business or taking this leadership role?

4. What achievements have you found the most satisfaction in doing?

5. To what do you attribute your current level of success?

6. How do you measure success? What does success look like to you?

7. What are the top five reasons a client should buy from you and not the competitors?

8. What are the top five reasons a company should hire or promote you?

9. What are two real-life examples where you or your team showed creativity and ingenuity?

10. What are two real-life examples where you or your team demonstrated critical thinking and were open-minded to trying new ways?

Weaknesses

1. What are two or three areas your staff or team members complain about the most?

2. What are two or three areas your clients or customers complain about the most?

3. Of the following areas, which ones do you do the poorest in: customer follow-up, timely billing, marketing, sales, being detailed oriented, customer satisfaction, empowering team members to make decisions, and so forth?

4. What does your competition do better than you??

5. Which areas do you, your employees, or partners procrastinate the most on?

6. How do you position your company in comparison to your competitor? (The cheapest, most expensive, generalist, specialist, small, big, focused, diverse, and so on.)

7. What do clients and outside partners say is your top strength?

Opportunities

1. Who are the people who already have a relationship with your potential clients? How can you start to build a relationship with them?

2. What are you doing to position your company as being on the cutting edge as a leader in the industry?

3. How could you better use the media to position yourself and your company as experts?

4. How could you take full advantage of:

    - Changes in technology (for example, online social networking websites, blogs, auto-responders, outsourcing, e-commerce)

    - Changes to the marketplace, both locally and nationally

    - Changes in social patterns, population movement, changing demographics, lifestyle changes, and so on

    - Changes in buying cycles and needs (faster turnaround time, lower prices, more selection, better quality, customization requests, and so on)

Threats

1. What are the five greatest obstacles your company or team currently faces?

2. How does rapidly changing technology affect your business model?

3. What are the current trends in your industry?

4. How does the economy affect your business for good or bad?

5. What are you currently doing to identify, train, and retain your top employees?

6. What would happen if your top three people were hired away by your most aggressive competitor?

7. How long would it take you to be up and running if your company was robbed or your building burned down?

8. What is the worst-case scenario you fear the most?

9. How can you better prepare to minimize the damage this would cause if it ever came true?

Questions for Deeper S-W-O-T Analysis

The following four questions are best used after you have already answered the earlier questions because they are based on comparing and contrasting two areas of the S-W-O-T grid to determine different strategies needed for success.

1. How can your strengths be leveraged to take advantage of developing opportunities? What are the strengths you will need to develop in the next 12 to 24 months to better position yourself or your company to profit from and quickly take advantage of new opportunities as they arise? **This is an S-O analysis, the upper tier of the S-W-O-T grid of Strengths and Opportunities.**

2. What specific ways can your strengths be used to counteract potential threats? How can you create an environment such that your team's creative thinking, ingenuity, and exceptional follow-through can flourish and not be diluted by perceived or real threats? **This is an S-T analysis, a cross tier of the S-W-O-T grid of Strengths and Threats.**

3. How can your weaknesses be overcome to tap into developing opportunities? What additional opportunities could you benefit from if you didn't have these weaknesses? What are two ways you could use delegation, outsourcing, or technology to minimize or

eliminate your weaknesses? **This is called a W-O analysis, a cross tier of the S-W-O-T grid of Weaknesses and Opportunities.**

4. Can you change your weaknesses by adding to or changing your team so that you can quickly counteract real threats? How does your team decide whether something is a real threat versus a perceived threat? How can you empower your team to take decisive action, instead of being paralyzed, in the face of a real threat? **This is called a W-T analysis, the bottom tier of the SWOT grid of Weaknesses and Threats.**

	Internal Reality	**External Reality**
Positive	Strengths	Opportunities
Negative	Weaknesses	Threats

* Fairley, Stephen, G and Zipp, William. **The Business Coaching Toolkit: Top 10 Strategies for Solving the Toughest Dilemmas Facing Organizations**. Hoboken, NJ: John Wiley & Sons, 2007.

Delegation

Delegation is the assignment of responsibility to another person to carry out specific activities. It is one of the core concepts of management leadership. The person who delegated the work still remains accountable for the outcome of the delegated work. Delegation in the beginning may be difficult and/or not an option. In time, however, you will find that you will not be able to perform all the tasks necessary to run your business. As you are "the face of your business", in the beginning, customers will want to interact with you directly. Furthermore, the priority of any business is to generate revenues (money). Though the "back office" work is important and necessary to get done, it is the revenue generation that allows that to happen. Everything starts with "closing the deal". If there are no deals closed there is no revenue coming in to the business. And if there is no revenue coming in, it does not matter how good your back office works or doesn't work.

Below is a business tool to help you with delegation. As with all tools in this handbook and in life, "use what you like and leave the rest". Having the right business tools is a very good starting point in your business. Some tools seem practical, and others may seem over the top, while other tools need to be customized to your specific needs. It's better to have more tools than less because you never know when a business situation may arise that you are not prepared for yet you have a tool to help you solve the problem which may be the difference in winning or losing a deal.

Getting Things Done Through Others

(Delegation Tool)

P-A-R: A New Approach to Delegation*

The secret to getting things done through others is having a system that allows both freedom and accountability. This system must be able to clarify expectations up front and provide opportunity for input from those involved in completing the task. There must also be flexibility in the system to allow for midcourse corrections, reworking the plans if necessary. That is the system we propose here captured in the acronym **P-A-R**.

P – Plan   A – Act with Authority   R – Review

The Cycle of Delegation

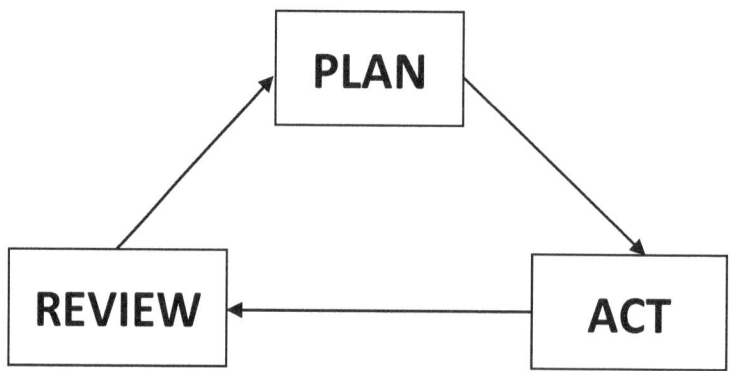

The P-A-R Delegation Flow Chart

P Plan	Co-create a **PLAN** for the task or project, setting clear Expectations **in writing** by answering these four questions: **WHO?** **WHAT?** **WHEN?** **HOW?** is going to do by and (and not how)
A Act with Authority	Free this person or group to **ACT with AUTHORITY** within a specified time frame, being available if needed. **AUTHORITY** **LEVELS:** Information Collaboration Execution **TIMEFRAME TO COMPLETE TASK(S)** 1 2 3 4 week/month weeks/months weeks/months weeks
R Review	Take time to **REVIEW** execution of the plan by asking three questions, making any necessary midcourse corrections. **PROGRESS?** **PROBLEMS?** **PLANS?** The Past The Present The Future

The P-A-R Delegation Worksheets

P - Plan

Task/Project Name: _____

Expectations: _____

_____

_____

_____

WHO?: _____

_____

_____

WHAT?: _____

_____

_____

WHEN?: _____

HOW?: _____

_____

_____

OR NOT HOW?: _____

_____

_____

The P-A-R Delegation Worksheets

A – Act with Authority

WHO?: _____

WHAT?: _____

AUTHORITY LEVELS: Information   Collaboration   Execution

TIMEFRAME TO COMPLETE TASK(S)

1	2	3	4
week/month	weeks/months	weeks/months	weeks

WHO?: _____

WHAT?: _____

AUTHORITY LEVELS: Information   Collaboration   Execution

TIMEFRAME TO COMPLETE TASK(S)

1	2	3	4
week/month	weeks/months	weeks/months	weeks/months

WHO?: _____

WHAT?: _____

AUTHORITY LEVELS: Information   Collaboration   Execution

TIMEFRAME TO COMPLETE TASK(S)

1	2	3	4
week/month	weeks/months	weeks/months	weeks/months

The P-A-R Delegation Worksheets

R - Review

WHO?: _____

WHAT?: _____

PROGRESS?: _____
The Past

_____

_____

_____

_____

PROBLEMS?: _____
The Present

_____

_____

_____

_____

PLANS?: _____
The Future

_____

_____

_____

_____

MORE ON GETTING THINGS DONE THROUGH OTHERS

- Begin with the WHO

- Help your WHO become His/Her Best

- Track the Things You Delegate

- Make Your Checkpoint Meetings Short

* Fairley, Stephen, G and Zipp, William. **The Business Coaching Toolkit: Top 10 Strategies for Solving the Toughest Dilemmas Facing Organizations**. Hoboken, NJ: John Wiley & Sons, 2007.

The Toolkit at www.MindTools.com

A website I would like to recommend is **www.MindTools.com**. MindTools.com teaches you the leadership, team management, problem-solving, personal productivity, and team-working skills that you need for a successful business/career. I suggest that you start with their free tools, which you can learn about on their website. If you find these useful, then subscribe to their free e-Newsletter. And, for the full Mind Tools career development experience, try their Mind Tools Club.

You can learn hundreds of useful business/career skills for free by visiting their **Toolkit** page, or by using the menu on all information pages. And by subscribing to their free e-Newsletter, you'll learn new business management and career techniques every week. This helps you make professional and personal development an ongoing part of your life, keeping your skills fresh and up-to-date.

D. Personal Life

1 - Plan your personal life the way you plan your professional life

Do not lose perspective on all parts of your life. It is very healthy to have a good "work life balance". In your business calendar, you should be planning your personal life "to do's" the same way you plan your professional (business) "to do's". By doing this it ensures that they will be attended to and completed. Life has a way of passing us by if we don't make time for the important things and people in our lives, both on a professional level and on a personable level.

2 – Have Fun! ☺

Another important thing to mention is to have fun doing all of these things! The amount of work can be daunting at times. Make your professional and personal days enjoyable! One nice thing about working for yourself is that you control your time. Every so often, take a long lunch, take a Tuesday afternoon, and make it Saturday afternoon instead, and make time for yourself after a major or even minor accomplishment. We all know what hard work looks like, but there is also a need to know what fun and relaxation looks like as well. Remember it's **always about balance**; too much of anything tends to put one out of balance. If you are going to work hard you might as well play hard as well! ☺

NOTES

PART VI:

Epilogue

Putting it All Together

NOTES

Chapter 30:

Your Life Purpose Statement –
Let the Whole World Know Who You Really Are!

What is Your Life Purpose Statement?

Your Life Purpose Statement is similar to a company's Mission Statement in that you are telling others what your life purpose is and how they can benefit by knowing and working with you. This is done for a number of reasons, one of which is to inform people what you do and how it can help them. We also live in a time that we need to let people know, in a short amount of time, what we do. This was discussed previously in this handbook when we spoke about the business networking introduction. In less than 2 minutes, which is the average attention span of adult, you tell people who you are and what you are looking for relative to employment or for seeking clients and how you can be of benefit to them or their business.

If we are talking about being of service and helping others and having others help us as well, if people don't understand what we do and the how it can benefit them, how can you expect others to understand and refer you and your work? Though many people may feel uncomfortable speaking about themselves, the truth is, if you don't inform people about what you do and how it can benefit them, **you are doing a disservice** to both the people that need your help and yourself. I meet many nice people that think it is improper to talk about themselves, when in fact, they can be helping others that need and want their help. **There is a huge difference between informing people about what you do and how it can be of help to them and bragging about oneself.** The Life Purpose Statement, presented in a proper, professional and courteous manner, is just the tool to tell people what you do in a non-threatening way and helping yourself at the same time.

Sample Life Purpose Statements

The main thing to keep in mind is to tell people what you do and how it **can benefit (help) them** and really what you are telling them is how it can benefit people in general. It does not have to be long, just informative. Think of your Life Purpose Statement as a conversation starter telling people in a short and precise statement what you are all about. Once the conversation gets going, then you can get into the details of what you do and how you do it. Your Life Purpose Statement is very similar to your business networking introduction, similar tools used in different ways. The Life Purpose Statement just tells people what your work is without expecting anything in return. In the business networking introduction, you are seeking to build relationships or find other contacts or whatever else is on your agenda.

Life Purpose Statements (Examples)

"As a **Life Purpose Coach** I help people find their true purpose in life so they can perform their true work and lead happy, prosperous and fulfilled lives."

"As a **Corporate Philanthropic Analyst** I help people with my work by ensuring my company makes wise and prudent decisions when sending our donations to help the right charities with their needs."

"As a **Baker** running my own business I help people gather together in my bakery where they can have a sense of community, talk, network and help one another with their needs."

"As a **Machinist** working in a factory I help people by performing quality work on the products I manufacture so people can enjoy their lives by using the products my company sells."

"As a **Mother/Father** I am ensuring my children eat right, get the proper amount of exercise and rest, know the difference between right and wrong so they can help build a better future for everyone."

Exercise: In this exercise you will be creating your Life Purpose Statement. First think about what you do, and then think about the benefits of what you do. Benefits are statements demonstrating how your services and/or products helps the person and/or people you are working with, as people always want to know what's in it for them.

1. What is/are the Service(s) and/or Product(s) to Deliver:

2. What is/are the Benefits from this/these Product(s) and Service(s)

3. Put it All Together Here

NOTES

NOTES

Chapter 31

Your Life Master Plan –
Planning Your Work and Working Your Plan

What is a Life Master Plan and Why Should You Write One?
A Life Master Plan simply stated is your blueprint to your goals, identifying how to achieve those goals and working those goals in realistic manner. This handbook has given you the tools, methods, and techniques to discover and achieve your life purpose (your true work). Now it's time to do some planning and then execution to achieve all your dreams, wants and desires. Your Life Master Plan does not need to be long or a drawn out dissertation; just a few pages just to keep you on track as what you need to be doing to achieve your goals.

In **Section One** clearly define your goals. How many goals should you define? Start with between three and seven. You want to make goals realistic and achievable (as stated in a previous chapter). What kind of goals should I be working on? What is important to you right now in your life? If you need clarity, remember the exercises you learned in the other chapters of the handbook of breathing and meditation. **You want goals to be specific, measurable, achievable, and realistic with a definitive time frame.** You also want your goals to be written, as writing, and reading your goals makes them more realistic. For example, "I would like to lose 26 pounds or more in 6 months and will begin this goal starting January 1, 2020 and ending June 30, 2020". Notice how the goal fits the criteria mentioned above; **specific** – How much weight? – 26 pounds or more**, measurable** – At the end of the 6 months I will weigh myself and see how much weight I have lost, **achievable** – it is advisable not to lose not more than one or two pounds of weight each week (and check with your doctor before starting any new weight lose regime) and **realistic** – if I eat right and exercise it is an achievable goal **with a definitive time frame – 6 months (26 weeks).**

In **Section Two** identify the process as to what you need to have and what you need to do in order to achieve your goals. Do you need to have certain skills and education to achieve your goals? Do you have them? Need to acquire them? Do they need to be acquired in a specific order and/or a specific timeframe? Really think about at a high level what it takes to achieve that goal. Using the previous example of weight loss once again; "In order for me to lose weight I will have to change my diet and join a gym to exercise on a regular basis". So in order to achieve that goal it will mean an investment of time and money to lose the weight that I have as my goal.

In **Section Three,** create a working plan for the items you have identified in Section One and Section Two. This is the day-to-day operation of the plan. What will need to do on a day to day, week to week and/or month to month basis to execute and complete your plan? Let's use the example we have been using in the previous two sections for weight loss. "In order to achieve my goal of losing 26 pounds in 6 month I will eat a daily diet of lean protein meats, plenty of fresh fruits and vegetables, drink a quart of water each day and walk one mile each day". Once a month look at your plan and see what's working, what needs improvement and what needs to be changed.

Just a reminder, the Life Master Plan does not have to be long and drawn out document; just a reminder to keep you on track to your goals and if you get off goals it is an easy way to get you back to achieving them. That's why you want to make your goals achievable, for once you get the taste for success in achieving the first, second and third goal there will be nothing standing in your way to achieve the life you desire. Start off small with goals that you can attain, then work your way up to larger and more important goals.

Exercise: Write Your Own Life Master Plan

1. Define Your Goals

2. Identify the Sections (One, Two, Three) and the Processes to Achieve Each Goal

3. Working Your Plan - Day to Day Execution of Goal:

NOTES

NOTES

Chapter 32

Enjoy and Celebrate Your Life's Purpose and Celebrate Your Life!

Celebrate Your Life Purpose!

Congratulations! You have discovered your life purpose and your true work. It has been a journey to get here and you finally made it! Now's it's time for a celebration! Do something good for yourself, spend a day at a health spa, go spend some time with some of your favorite people. You've earned it!

On a more serious note, it is quite an achievement to have clearly defined your life purpose and have concrete steps to implement and live your life purpose to live a happier, prosperous and personally fulfilling life.

Be Good to Yourself - All You Need is Love...

Love - we all want it, yet how many people have it and are willing to give it away? It all starts with the individual loving oneself. Not physical love of the body, but love of the spirit. You must first have love for yourself, for how can you give away something to others that you do not have for yourself? We have love for other people, animals, inanimate objects and even food but do we have a healthy love of ourselves?

Love can be so misunderstood at times. Some people think of romantic love, others think of physical love and yet others think of a narcissistic type of love. But can there be love just for love's sake? Can we love the person and not the body they inhabit? Of course we can. This is evident in all the major religions, spiritual traditions and their respective prophets, saints, and angels. **Love is love.** When there is true love, a pure love, a real love, a healthy love, a love that transcends all space and time between people, who is to judge whether it is right or wrong? Only the Creator is to be that judge.

Love is Healing

The emotion of love is so strong. It can heal mind, spirit and some feel the body as well. It is a force so strong it cannot be denied. The love a parent has for a child transcends all space and all time. It is a love with no ending, even when the body is no longer here, the love lives on. True love never dies.

Studies have shown that babies, who are not touched, do not develop properly. While those who are touched develop faster and are often discharged quicker from the hospital. The power of love has the ability to heal on so many different levels. **Though we cannot see love we know it when we feel it.** The power of love transcends all. Love is a universal emotion in the world. Is the love of one's child different from someone who is rich versus someone who is poor? Is the love of one's child different for people of color, ethnic or religious backgrounds? Is the love one's child different in different parts of the world? No, it is not. **Love is love.**

The More You Give Love the More Love You Get

The funny thing about the gift of love is the more you give the more you get. It is though there is a natural law that you if give love you get more in return. Love is such a powerful emotion, yet why are so many people afraid to give love, show love, and receive love? The source of love is endless. You can give love and yet you will find even more love to give. It is an amazing emotion the Creator has given humankind, the gift of love.

So many gifts of human kind are free to give and yet priceless to receive. By demonstrating love to another person, both the giver and receiver are positively affected. Studies show the simple act of touching another, raises the serotonin level in the brain. Serotonin refers to a natural hormone that is produced by the body. Serotonin is produced in the pineal gland, which is part of the human brain. Research also suggests that touch deprivation in early development and again in adolescence may contribute to violence in adults. Further studies have found that a culture in which there was more physical affection toward young children had lower rates of adult physical violence, and vice versa. Furthermore, the amount of touching that occurs in different cultures is highly variable. Other studies have found that in touching behavior in several countries, couples were observed sitting in cafes for 30-minute periods, and the amount of touching between them was recorded. Among the highest touch cultures was France (110 times per 30 minutes), while the U.S. was among the lowest (2 times per 30 minutes).

Interestingly, high-touch cultures have relatively low rates of violence, and low-touch cultures have extremely high rates of youth and adult violence.

When your life is full of love you truly are prosperous indeed. Love has a way of making you and those around you very, very prosperous!

Celebrate Your Life Purpose with Others Through Service - Helping Others Through Public Service

Though mentioned earlier in this handbook, it is worth mentioning again, especially in these trying times. Many people feel the need and desire to help others. A good way to do this is through public service. Public service can be helping others in a myriad of different ways. By serving the public you may be working with people directly in a one-on-one manner, in groups or helping humankind in its entirety.

You are truly prosperous when you help others. As you help others you are sharing your prosperity. When you share your prosperity, it will come back to you many, many times over!

Chapter 33

Now Let's Get Back to Our Better New, Better and Prosperous Lives!

You now have many tools in your "Life Toolkit" to be prosperous in your professional and personal life and start a new and better life. After the pandemic it will be unlikely that life will be "business as usual" and that there may even be a new way(s) of living life. I suspect the basics of daily life will be the same. Work – will always be work, be it showing up at a place of business (and how that may look after the pandemic), working remotely and possibly a combination of both, if the type of work you do lends it self to being so. One new reality of the post pandemic world is that many jobs will be gone, eliminated, and/or no longer needed. That's why it's very important that you understand **_all_** of your skills and education and how you can help businesses (or whatever your choice is for earning a living) with their problems. The more you understand how to solve the problems of your prospective employers and/or the marketplace you are seeking, the more valuable you will be to those that need your skills and education and they will seek you out for your help. However, as I previously mentioned, it is YOUR RESPONSIBILITY to tell the world what you can do for them and how you can help them. Once you understand the problems of the marketplace you are seeking to become a part of, then you can show that marketplace how you can help them with your background, you will be in demand. Also, remember the ability to learn many new things with the internet based teaching resources that are available which will make you even more valuable to the marketplace.

It will be time to reintegrate back to the world in whatever manner that is appropriate for you, be it back into the workforce, running your own business, a new career path, retirement, a combination of all that is being mentioned or whatever is appropriate for you and your family. While the pandemic has been and continues to be a tragic event in so many different ways (lives lost, families torn apart, business and finances ruined, etc.), we must do our best to start over again and begin a new and better way of life. In certain ways, life may be radically different than it was before the pandemic and in other ways, it may be similar to the ways things were before. Whatever it may be a new way of life and living will be created and it can be even better than it was before. As for the concept of a "new normal", personally, I will just call it a "new" way of living.

Getting back to our lives, presents tremendous opportunities to all of us to have better and more prosperous lives than we had before. It has been amazing how all of humankind has banded together to help those that need help and the compassion being shown by so many people, especially the first responders and those in the medical field is nothing short of miraculous. There are many new opportunities being created in a post-pandemic world and yes, it involves change, but nothing of significance ever happen without change. Yes, new skills and educations may need to be acquired to meet the new opportunities, but the exciting part is that there **will be** new opportunities available and you can go as far as your talents will take you.

NOTES

Conclusion

As I get to the close of this handbook as to the pandemic is ever so slowly winding down, it brings to my mind that there will always be endings and new beginnings in a person's life. Some will be major (lose of livelihood, finances, house, etc.) and some will be minor. Starting over is not easy**,** but if you have the proper state of mind, the proper tools and support you can start over and build a new life even better than the one you once had before. No it may not be easy, but it can be done, and you can do it.

Let's review all that you have learned in this handbook. We started with

Part I: The Prologue – The Game Plan and understanding the reality of starting over especially if you have suffered a major loss – be it finances, career, housing, and/or all of the aforementioned.

Next in **Part II: The Spiritual (Our Life Force)** we examined the importance of spirituality in one's life and how unseen forces can help support us on starting a new and better life.

In **Part III: The Emotional (Our Emotional Heart)** we need to make sure nothing emotionally is holding us back from making a fresh start and if there are emotional issues we need to deal with them so we can make room for the prosperity that is waiting for us. If you're carrying "emotional baggage" around with you, where are you going to put your "prosperity luggage" when it does arrive? Having good, healthy and loving relationships with ourselves and the people in our lives; family, friends, co-workers, and even other people in society, as well as the animals is another important aspect of being prosperous.

In **Part IV: The Mental (Our Mind)** we have to view and use our minds like a very important "mental computer" (which it is) and learn how to use it, exercise it and relax it properly so we can be at our "mental best" when working, dealing with others and reaching our new goals.

In **Part V: The Physical (Our Body)** we must take care of our physical bodies to make all the prosperity in our lives happen; eating right, exercising, and becoming a productive member of society once again. You have learned job search techniques to get an even better job than you had before and/or how to start a new business (and associated business plans and business tools).

In **Part VI: The Epilogue – Putting it All Together** we're doing just that. We are all here for a specific reason. A specific a life purpose – whether your life purpose is to cure cancer, raise a family or just making the world a better place for everyone. Make it happen! What's YOUR Life Purpose and what's your Life Purpose Plan to make it happen? And when you do make it happen, enjoy and share the fruits of your labors!

Part VII: Resources are websites and various tools to help you find a better job, build a business, a Book List to fill your mind with good stuff to be inspired to be a better person and make the world a better place.

As I finish this handbook, the world is slowly opening up again in phases. Though it's too early for all the statistics to be coming in on lives lost, jobs lost, closed businesses, mounting debts and so on, one thing is very clear, things are not the same. There is much suffering on all levels – spiritually, emotionally, mentally, physically, and financially. Things will be far from being the same. I suspect life as we knew it will not be the same again. However, we as people will endure, adapt and will be prosperous**,** but I strongly suspect it will look different. Hopefully, it will look, feel and be different in a much better way for all people. But it will be different…

I do want to reiterate the quote form the late, great and famous actress Elizabeth Taylor; *"You just do it. You force yourself to get up. You force yourself to put one foot in front of the other, and God d--n it, you refuse to let it get to you. You fight. You cry. You curse. Then you go about the business of living. That's how I've done it. There's no other way".* Yes, I'm using Elizabeth Taylor's quote again. It just fits, is helpful and for some of us (including myself), it's just the plain truth! And the truth will set you free! Remember, rest if you must, but don't you quit!

This may be the end of this handbook, but it's the beginning of a whole new world for all of us. A world of all types of prosperity – spiritually, emotionally, mentally, physically, ,and financially. Nothing beats the freedom to do whatever you want to do and go as far as your talents will take you in a free and democratic society. It may be the ending of one chapter in your life, but it's a whole new chapter and a new beginning in a brand new world. You have the tools, talent, and internal and external resources to make it happen, so go lead your best life for yourself, family, friends, and society. The best is yet to be!

NOTES

NOTES

PART VII:

Resources

NOTES

Resources

1. Job Search Resources

- Career Sherpa. **Best Websites for 2020 Job Search.** https://careersherpa.net/best-websites-for-2020-job-search/

- CareerSidekick. **The Top 10 Job Search Engines For 2020.** https://careersidekick.com/tools/job-search-websites/

- Robert Half Job Seeker. **25 Best Job Search Websites.** https://www.roberthalf.com/blog/job-market/10-best-job-search-websites

- Indeed Career Guide. **10 Job Searching Resources.** https://www.indeed.com/career-advice/finding-a-job/job-searching-resources

- Monster.com. **Job Search, Career Advice and Hiring Resources.** https://www.monster.com/

- Refdesk.com. **JOB SEARCH RESOURCES (Over 80 resources).** https://www.refdesk.com/jobsearch.html

- The Jub. **7 Best Job Search Engines for Millennials | Top Job Boards 2020**. https://www.thejub.com/millennial-career-resources/2018/9/24/7-best-job-search-engines-for-millennials

- CareerOnestop. **Your source for career exploration, training and jobs. Sponsored by the U.S. Department of Labor.** https://www.careeronestop.org/

- AARP.org. **Job Search Resources for 50+.** https://www.aarp.org/work/job-hunting/info-06-2009/job_search_resources.html

- Dice.com. **Finding Jobs in Tech.** https://www.dice.com/

- LinkedIn.com. **LinkedIn Job Search: Find US Jobs, Internships, Jobs Near Me.** https://www.linkedin.com/jobs/

- The Balance Careers. **Tips for Using Google for Job Searches.** https://www.thebalancecareers.com/google-for-jobs-4140171

2. Small Business Resources

Web sites and Resources for
the Small Business Owner/Operator:

Amazon.com
Find the book you need from millions in stock.
http://www.amazon.com/exec/obidos/redirect-home/smallbusinessr05

American Express Small Business Network
Ideas, information and money-saving benefits from American Express.
http://www.americanexpress.com/homepage/smallbusiness.shtml?

Brenner Information Group
Valuable books on pricing various desktop publishing services
http:// www.brennerbooks.com.

Best of Sites
Links to hundreds of content-rich sites in 50 different business categories from accounting to writing
http://www.bestofsites.com

Business Start-Up Guide for Young Entrepreneurs
What young entrepreneurs need to know to start a business
https://www.ignitespot.com/business-startup-guide-for-young-entrepreneurs

Capital Connection

The entrepreneur's resource for finance: where to find money, marketing advisers, business-plan consultants and more

http://www.capital-connection.com

CCH Business Owner's Toolkit

Cut costs, increase productivity with downloadable checklists, interactive employment tools and more

http://www.toolkit.cch.com

Center for Women's Business Research

Conducts studies and surveys of female entrepreneurs, their management practices, financing sources and more

http://www.cwbr.org

Entreworld

The Kauffman Center for Entrepreneurial Leadership offers articles, tips and more for starting and building a successful business.

http://www.entreworld.org

Entrepreneur.com

Entrepreneur Media offers information, services and advice for small-business owners

http://www.entrepreneur.com

Federal Contracting Made Easy

CPA Scott Stanberry at Management Concepts has written a book that is sure to help anyone who wants to win federal contracts. Who can pass up such opportunities in this economy?

http://www.managementconcepts.com

Financial Literacy

To be financially literate is to know how to manage your money. This means learning how to pay your bills, how to borrow and save money responsibly, and how and why to invest and plan for retirement.
https://www.annuity.org/financial-literacy/

Garage Technology Ventures

Information for people starting their businesses in their garages, slanted toward technology companies and others seeking venture funding
http://www.garage.com

Harris InfoSource

Profiles of 750,000 companies from manufacturing, technology and service sectors. invaluable for business planning research, sales and marketing and more. Fees apply.
http://www.harrisinfo.com

Home Business Journal

Directory of home business, articles, advice for people running businesses from home
http://www.homebizjour.com

Home Business Magazine

Online edition of publication for home-business entrepreneurs and telecommuters
http://www.homebusinessmag.com

Hugh Hewitt

Small business owners who ignore politics do so at their own peril. Hugh Hewitt is an author, television commentator and syndicated radio talk-show host heard in more than 40 markets nationwide. At his web site learn about important political issues and find a local station that broadcasts his radio programs.

http://www.hughhewitt.com

Idea Cafe

Ideas and information about planning, financing, starting and running a small business.

http://www.ideacafe.com

Library Online

Looking for letter templates; prewritten, customizable business letters; valuable tips for writing business letters? This is the place.

http://www.libraryonline.com

My Own Business

A free, online 12-session course that provides the basics for entrepreneurs. This site has plenty of help for both start-ups and already operating ventures

http://www.myownbusiness.org

National Association for the Self-Employed

More than half the businesses in America are run by the self-employed. Get information, insurance and more.

http://www.nase.org

National Association of Women Business Owners
Premier organization for women entrepreneurs with chapters nationwide
http://www.nawbo.org

National Federation of Independent Business
News, views and tools on politics and business management from the small-business advocate with 600,000 members from every industry.
http://www.nfib.com

Out of Your Mind and Into the Marketplace
Write the best business plan for guiding growth and success and for finding capital for your business
http://www.business-plan.com

Profit Dynamics
Partners Brian E. Hill and Dee Power are authors of "Inside Secrets to Venture Capital" and "Attracting Capital from Angles: How Their Money and Their Experience Can Help You Build a Successful Company."
http://www.capital-connection.com

Publicity Insider
Designed for small businesses and entrepreneurs, PublicityInsider.com contains the latest how-to PR techniques, Internet promotion strategies, editorial opportunities, press release samples and more.
http://www.PublicityInsider.com

QuickBooks Users

QuickBooks is the top accounting software for small businesses. This site offers plenty of help for small business owners, independent bookkeepers, accountants and accounting clerks.
http://www.QuickbooksUsers.com

SCORE

Service Corps of Retired Executives, with chapters nationwide, provides free business counseling in person or online
http://www.score.org.

Small Business Administration

The federal agency that works with small-business owners, providing hundreds of articles on start-up, financing, management and government contracting
http://www.sba.gov

SmallBusiness.com

Articles, advice and recommendations for small-business owners
http://www.smallbusiness.com

Small Business Insurance Center-The Hartford

The site explains the different types of coverage for small businesses, translates dense insurance jargon into plain English and provides tools to help analyze specific coverage needs, minimize risk and even develop a disaster recovery plan.
http://sb.thehartford.com

SOHO

Small Office Home Office professionals share information on marketing, finance and technology

http://www.soho.org

U.S. Legal Forms

Offers wide variety of legal forms from incorporation documents to bill of sale to contracts.

http://www.uslegalforms.com

Work at Home Directory

Extensive resource for products, services and information catering to home and Internet-based businesses

http://www.thisbizis4u.com

Young Entrepreneurs Organization

Global, nonprofit educational organization for entrepreneurs under 40 whose companies have annual revenues of at least $1 million.

http://www.yeo.org

NOTES

Internet Based Education and Training

1. G2: Best Online Course Providers - https://www.g2.com/categories/online-course-providers

2. Online Schools: Your Guide to Accredited Online Schools - https://www.OnlineSchools.org/

3. Class Central: Make Informed Online Learning Decisions - www.ClassCentral.com/

4. The Top Online College and Courses Online - www.OnlineCourses.com

5. COURSERA: Build skills with courses, certificates, and degrees online from world-class universities and companies - https://www.Coursera.org/

6. OPEN EDUCATION DATAbase: OEDb is a comprehensive online education directory for both free and for-credit learning options - https://OEDb.org/

7. Training Industry: Top Online Learning Library Companies - https://trainingindustry.com/top-training-companies/e-learning/2019-top-online-learning-library-companies/

8. EDX: edX is the trusted platform for education and learning - https://www.edx.org/

NOTES

Book List

- **How to Win Friends and Influence People** by Dale Carnegie
- **The Magic of Thinking Big** by David Schwartz
- **Man's Search for Meaning** by Viktor Frankel
- **Think and Grow Rich** by Napoleon Hill
- **The One Minute Manager** by Kenneth Blanchard
- **Awaken The Giant Within** by Anthony Robbins
- **Screw It Lets Do It: Lessons in Life** by Richard Branson
- **The Art of Happiness** by Dalai Lama
- **The Four Agreements** by Don Miguel Ruiz
- **Reinventing the Body, Resurrecting the Soul: How to Create A New You** by Deepak Chopra
- **The Greatest Salesman In The World** by Og Mandino
- **Switch: How to Change Things When Change is Hard** by Chip & Dan Heath
- **The Gifts of Imperfection** by Brene Brown
- **Meditations** by Marcus Aurelius
- **Willpower** by John Tierney Roy Baumeister
- **The 7 Habits of Highly Effective People** by Stephen Covey
- **Mini Habits** by Stephen Guise
- **Make It Stick** by Peter C. Brown, Henry Roediger, Mark McDaniel

NOTES

Footnotes

[1] USAGov. *After a Disaster.* Retrieved from https://www.usa.gov/after-disaster

[2] Steinhilber, Brianna. (2018). *Is your emotional baggage holding you back?.* Retrieved from https://www.nbcnews.com/better/health/your-emotional-baggage-holding-you-back-ncna877596

[3] Følling, Ingrid S., Solbjør, Marit and Helvik, Anne S. (2015). *Previous experiences and emotional baggage as barriers to lifestyle change - a qualitative study of Norwegian Healthy Life Centre participants.* Retrieved from https://www.ncbi.nlm.nih.gov/pmc/articles/PMC4476174/

[4] Green, Daniel J. (2018). *I followed the federal dietary and exercise guidelines for a year.* Here's what happened. Retrieved from https://www.nbcnews.com/better/health/i-followed-federal-dietary-exercise-guidelines-year-these-are-results-ncna869331

[5] Compton, Julie. (2018). *Why 'keystone habits' can help you transform your life one small step at a time.* Retrieved from https://www.nbcnews.com/better/pop-culture/why-keystone-habits-can-help-you-transform-your-life-one-ncna877101

[6] Steinhilber, Brianna. (2018). *6 strategies to take your career to the next level this year.* Retrieved from https://www.nbcnews.com/better/business/6-strategies-take-your-career-next-level-year-ncna836311

NOTES

Bibliography

- Boehman, Jonathan and Weigelt, David. **Dot Boom: Marketing to Baby Boomers Through Meaningful Online Engagement.** Great Falls, VA: LINX Corp., 2009.

- D'Aversa, Oreste J., *Healing the Holes in My Soul: How I Saved My Own Life, Became Whole to Lead a Happy, Fulfilling and Joyous Life!* New Jersey: Cutting Edge Technology Publishing, 2020.

- D'Aversa, Oreste J., **SELLING for NON-SELLING PROFESSIONALS ©***: Learn Basic, Proven and Results Oriented Sales Skills, Methods and Techniques to Get Clients Consistently with No Prior Sales Background and Increase Revenues, Reduce Business Stress and Create a Productive Work-Life Balance!* New Jersey: Cutting Edge Technology Publishing, 2019.

- D'Aversa, Oreste J., **BABY BOOMER ENTREPRENEUR:** *Implementing the Boomer Business Success System© The Complete and Proven Guide to Starting a Successful Business, having Financial Freedom with the Lifestyle that You Want While Making a Difference in the World!* New Jersey: Cutting Edge Technology Publishing, 2016.

- D'Aversa, Oreste J., *Discovery Your Life Purpose: The Journey Within – The True Guide to Achieving Happiness, Prosperity and Personal Fulfillment.* New Jersey: Cutting Edge Technology Publishing, 2010.

- D'Aversa, Oreste J., *The Seven Simple Principles of Prosperity: Practical exercises to Achieve a Rich, Happy and Joyous Life!* New Jersey: Cutting Edge Technology Publishing, 2005.

- D'Aversa, Oreste J., *The Resume Writing Kit: How to Write the Last Resume You Will Ever Need!* New Jersey: Cutting Edge Technology Publishing, 2004.

- Fairley, Stephen, G and Zipp, William. **The Business Coaching Toolkit: Top 10 Strategies for Solving the Toughest Dilemmas Facing Organizations**. Hoboken, NJ: John Wiley & Sons, 2007.

- Hicks, Esther and Hicks, Jerry. **The Law of Attraction: The Basics of the Teachings of Abraham** ™ Carlsbad, CA: Hay House. 2006.

Services Available:

If you would like assistance getting started on your new post pandemic journey, I offer Coaching, Consulting and Training services, so there is no need to go it alone. You can learn more about the services mention by going to the following websites:

www.LifeBeyondTheCoronavirus.com

www.MetroSmallBusinessCoaching.com

NOTES

The Phoenix

The spiritual meaning of the mythical bird The Phoenix. The Phoenix represents transformation and rebirth in its fire. As a powerful spiritual totem, the phoenix is the ultimate symbol of strength and renewal.

I created the symbol below from my own personal rebirth I now gift it to you. Find your own internal Phoenix it's inside of you. It's inside of all of us.

If you enjoyed the book...

You might want to learn more about the:

- **Training Class (On-Line)**

- **Coaching (Guidance)**

- **Consulting (Deliverables)**

Learn more about the above and more by going to:

www.LifeBeyondThePandemic.com

Wishing you much success, joy, and a prosperous life!